my **revisi**

A2 Edexcel History

FROM KAISER TO FÜHRER

GERMANY, 1900–45

Barbara Warnock

Series editors:
Robin Bunce
Laura Gallagher

The publishers would like to thank the following for permission to reproduce copyright material:

Acknowledgements

Richard J. Evans: extracts from *The Third Reich in Power, 1933–1939* (Allen Lane/The Penguin Press, 2005), reproduced by permission of the publisher; **Niall Ferguson:** extracts from *The War of the World: History's Age of Hatred* (Penguin Books, 2006), © Niall Ferguson, 2006, reproduced by permission of Penguin Books Ltd; **David G. Herrmann:** extracts from *The Arming of Europe and the Making of the First World War* (Princeton University Press, 1996), © Princeton University Press, reprinted by permission of Princeton University Press; **Ian Kershaw:** extracts from *The 'Hitler Myth'. Image and Reality in the Third Reich* (Oxford University Press, 1987), reproduced by permission of Oxford University Press, www.oup.com; **H. W. Koch:** extracts from Imanuel Geiss, from *Origins of the First World War* (Macmillan, 1972), reproduced by permission of Palgrave Macmillan; **James Joll and Gordon Martell:** extracts from *The Origins of the First World War, 3/e* (Pearson Education, 2007), reproduced by permission of the publisher.

Every effort has been made to trace all copyright holders, but if any have been inadvertently overlooked the Publishers will be pleased to make the necessary arrangements at the first opportunity.

Although every effort has been made to ensure that website addresses are correct at time of going to press, Hodder Education cannot be held responsible for the content of any website mentioned in this book. It is sometimes possible to find a relocated web page by typing in the address of the home page for a website in the URL window of your browser.

Hachette UK's policy is to use papers that are natural, renewable and recyclable products and made from wood grown in sustainable forests. The logging and manufacturing processes are expected to conform to the environmental regulations of the country of origin.

Orders: please contact Bookpoint Ltd, 130 Milton Park, Abingdon, Oxon OX14 4SB.
Telephone: +44 (0)1235 827720. Fax: +44 (0)1235 400454. Lines are open 9.00a.m.–5.00p.m., Monday to Saturday, with a 24-hour message answering service. Visit our website at www.hoddereducation.co.uk.

© Barbara Warnock 2013
First published in 2013 by
Hodder Education,
an Hachette UK company
338 Euston Road
London NW1 3BH
Impression number 10 9 8 7 6 5 4
Year 2017 2016 2015 2014

Cover photo © Stephen Mulcahey/Alamy

Typeset in 11/13 Stempel Schneidler Std-Light by Datapage (India) Pvt. Ltd.
Artwork by Datapage
Printed in Spain
A catalogue record for this title is available from the British Library
ISBN 978 1 444 177671

Contents

Introduction

About Unit 3

Unit 3 is worth 60 per cent of your A2 level. It requires detailed knowledge of a historical period and the ability to explore and analyse the interpretations of historians. Overall, 34 per cent of the marks available are awarded for source analysis (Assessment Objective 2), and 66 per cent for using your own knowledge to form an explanation (Assessment Objective 1).

In the exam, you are required to answer one question with two parts. Part (a) is worth 30 marks and Part (b) is worth 40 marks. It is advisable to spend approximately two-fifths of your time in the exam on Part (a) and the remaining three-fifths on Part (b). There will be a choice of two questions in both Part (a) and Part (b). You must answer one Part (a) and one Part (b) question.

Part (a) focuses on AO1. It will test your ability to:

■ select information that focuses on the question

■ organise this information to provide an answer to the question

■ show range and depth in the examples you provide

■ analyse the significance of the information used to reach an overall judgement.

Part (b) focuses on both AO1 and AO2. It will test your ability to:

■ select information that focuses on the question

■ organise this information to provide an answer to the question

■ identify the interpretations provided by the sources

■ weigh the interpretations of the sources, and integrate these interpretations with evidence from your own knowledge to reach an overall judgement.

From Kaiser to Führer: Germany, 1900–45

The exam board specifies that students should study four general areas which will be examined in Part (a):

1. The Second Reich, 1900–1919: politics, economics, society and the impact of the First World War

2. Weimar Germany: early crises, 'Golden Years' and culture

3. The origins and rise of the Nazis, 1919–33

4. Germany during the Second World War, 1939–1945: opposition and conformity, anti-Semitism and the evolution of the 'Final Solution', and the efficiency of the war economy.

In addition, the exam board specifies that students should study two historical controversies which will be examined in Part (b):

1. The extent to which Germany was responsible for the outbreak of the First World War

2. The extent to which the Nazi regime enjoyed popular support and rested on the consent of the German people, and the extent to which the Nazi state was efficient and carried out Hitler's will.

How to use this book

This book has been designed to help you to develop the knowledge and skills necessary to succeed in this exam. The book is divided into six sections – one for each general area of the course. Each section is made up of a series of topics organised into double page spreads. On the left-hand page, you will find a summary of the key content you need to learn. Words in bold in the key content are defined in the glossary. On the right-hand page, you will find exam-focused activities. Together, these two strands of the book will take you through the knowledge and skills essential for exam success.

There are three levels of exam-focused activities:

■ Band 1 activities are designed to develop the foundational skills needed to pass the exam.

■ Band 2 activities are designed to build on the skills developed in Band 1 activities and to help you achieve a C grade.

■ Band 3 activities are designed to enable you to access the highest grades.

Each section ends with an exam-style question and model A grade answer with examiner's commentary. This should give you guidance on what is required to achieve the top grades.

Section 1: The Second Reich – society and government in Germany, c.1900–1919

The constitution of the Second Reich

German unification, 1871

The Second Reich is the name given to the unified German state that was established following **Prussia's** victory in the Franco-Prussian War 1870–1871. German-speaking states, with the exception of the Austrian Empire, unified under Prussian dominance. These states had previously been connected by a **customs union** and now they came together in a political and military union with the Prussian king as Emperor or Kaiser of Germany.

> **Prussia**
>
> Established in 1525, Prussia was a German state that rose in power and status through the eighteenth and nineteenth centuries. Following German unification, Prussia comprised 65 per cent of the surface area of unified Germany and 62 per cent of its population. Consequently, Prussia dominated the Second Reich.

The constitution

The architect of both German unification and the constitution of the Second Reich was the dominant German politician of his age, Otto von Bismarck. Of Prussian origin, Bismarck sought to protect the power of Prussia and the Prussian ruling elite in his constitution, while allowing an element of popular democracy. The powers and role of each part of the political system of the Second Reich are outlined below. You will see how the constitution operated in practice later on in this section.

The Kaiser

The Kaiser, who constitutionally had to be the Prussian monarch, was **sovereign** in the Second Reich and the constitution granted him significant powers. The Kaiser was Commander-in-Chief of the army and in charge of foreign policy. The Kaiser appointed and could dismiss the Chancellor (Prime Minister) and government ministers. The Kaiser could also **dissolve** the Reichstag (parliament) and was president of the **Bundesrat (federal** council). Germany was ruled by Kaiser Wilhelm II from 1888 to 1918.

The Chancellor and the ministers

The Chancellor was responsible for presenting **legislation** to parliament and the Chancellor and ministers implemented laws. The Chancellor and ministers were not accountable to parliament, only to the Kaiser. Kaiser Wilhelm II tended to appoint members of the Prussian aristocracy, the *Junkers*, to these positions.

The Reichstag

The Reichstag, or parliament, was the democratic element of the German constitution, as its members were elected. All men over the age of 25 had the vote. The Reichstag could vote to accept, reject or amend legislation.

The Bundesrat (federal council)

The Bundesrat contained representatives appointed by regional state assemblies and along with the Reichstag also held legislative powers. The Bundesrat could initiate legislation and if fourteen or more members of the Bundesrat voted against a law it could be **vetoed**. Bismarck engineered the composition of this body to ensure the dominance of Prussian **conservatives**. Many of the powers of the Kaiser were supposed to be shared with the Bundesrat, but the composition of the council meant that Kaiser Wilhelm II was able to control it.

The federal state

To reflect the independent origins of parts of the newly unified Germany, the constitution was a federal one, within which individual states had considerable powers to determine the nature of their local political arrangements and to run education, health care and local policing.

The army

The German army was accountable only to the Kaiser and swore an oath of allegiance to him and not to the government.

Complete the paragraph

Below are a sample Part (a) exam-style question and a paragraph written in answer to this question. The paragraph contains a point and a concluding explanatory link back to the question, but lacks examples. Complete the paragraph adding examples in the space provided.

'The constitution of the Second Reich was fundamentally undemocratic in nature.' How far do you agree with this opinion?

> The role of the Kaiser within the constitution of the Second Reich was evidence that the constitution was fundamentally undemocratic in nature. For example,
>
> _____
>
> _____
>
> _____
>
> _____
>
> In this way, the role of the Kaiser indicates that the constitution of the Second Reich was fundamentally undemocratic because the Kaiser had great power which was unaccountable to the German people.

Eliminate irrelevance

Below are a sample Part (a) exam-style question and a paragraph written in answer to this question. Read the paragraph and identify parts of the paragraph that are not directly relevant to the question. Draw a line through the information that is irrelevant and justify your deletions in the margin.

'The constitution of the Second Reich was fundamentally undemocratic in nature.' How far do you agree with this opinion?

> The Reichstag, or Parliament, was clearly the most democratic element of the constitution of the Second Reich, which created a federal state. The Reichstag was designed by Bismarck following Prussia's victory in the Franco-Prussian War, to give the German people a voice in the German government. Otto von Bismarck himself was of Prussian origin, and therefore favoured the Prussians. The Reichstag was elected by all men over the age of 25 and had the power to reject, accept and amend any law. Prior to the creation of the constitution, Germany had been little more than a customs union dominated by Prussia. However, there were limits to the power of the Reichstag. For example, the German army was accountable to the Kaiser only and therefore the elected representatives in the Reichstag could exercise no control over the army. Overall, the Reichstag is evidence that the constitution of the Second Reich was not fundamentally undemocratic in nature because, through control of the Reichstag, the German people could affect legislation. However, this democratic aspect of the constitution was deliberately limited and therefore it is impossible to argue that the constitution of the Second Reich was wholly democratic.

Economic and social developments

Germany's rapid economic expansion between 1890 and 1914 had important social and political repercussions for the Second Reich.

Economic developments

- **Economic growth:** Germany's economic growth was exceptional between 1890 and 1914: on average the economy expanded by 4.5 per cent a year. Coal and iron production almost doubled in these years and, by 1914, Germany's share of world trade was equal to that of Britain. Germany's steel industry (dominated by the massive Krupp Corporation) was particularly strong: German steel production exceeded that of Britain by 1900.

- **New industries:** Germany excelled in industries that used new and innovative technologies, such as chemicals, pharmaceuticals, electrics and motor manufacture. Daimler and Diesel developed cars, while AEG and Siemens became huge electrical businesses: by 1913, Germany produced around 50 per cent of the world's electrical goods. In chemicals, Germany led the world in the production of synthetic dyes and pharmaceuticals and in precision engineering. The production of optics and mechanical goods sectors also expanded significantly.

- **An industrial economy:** These economic developments resulted in a growing proportion of the population working in the industrial and service sectors of the economy. The contribution that industry made to the country's GNP rose from around 33 per cent to 42 per cent.

- **Improved transport infrastructure:** Germany's transport network also developed at this time with trains, tramways and trolley buses constructed to facilitate travel and industrial development.

Social consequences

- **Urbanisation:** A population boom and new jobs and opportunities in industry stimulated urbanisation: by 1910, 60 per cent of the population lived in urban areas, the highest rate in Europe. The populations of Breslau, Cologne, Dresden, Hamburg, Leipzig and Munich all exceeded half a million by 1910, while Berlin had in excess of 2 million inhabitants. Overcrowding and homelessness were negative consequences of this population shift, but the development of an effective transport infrastructure helped to alleviate problems.

- **Poor standards of living:** Despite low unemployment and increases in average wages, the standard of living for most working people was low and conditions at work poor. Discontent about this created a boom in membership of trade unions: over 3 million people were members by 1913.

- **Class tensions:** Industrialisation in Germany produced heightened tensions. The industrial **working class** were sometimes in conflict with the owners of industry over pay and conditions at work. The *Junker* elite were keen to conserve their dominant position in society and, in common with the owners of industry, were concerned about the growth of **socialism**. The lower middle class, or *Mittelstand* (small traders, shopkeepers and artisans), were often discontented, as they found their living standard threatened by new industries. In the countryside, competition from Canada and the USA squeezed the peasantry and farmers.

Simple essay style

Below is a sample Part (a) exam-style question. Use your own knowledge and the information on the opposite page to produce a plan for this question. Choose four general points, and provide three pieces of specific information to support each general point. Once you have planned your essay, write the introduction and conclusion for the essay. The introduction should list the points to be discussed in the essay. The conclusion should summarise the key points and justify which point was the most important.

To what extent did economic developments in Germany in the period 1900–1914 pose a threat to the power of the elites?

Spectrum of significance

Below are a sample Part (a) exam-style question and a list of general points which could be used to answer the question. Use your own knowledge and the information on the opposite page to reach a judgement about the importance of these general points to the question posed. Write numbers on the spectrum below to indicate their relative importance. Having done this, write a brief justification of your placement, explaining why some of these factors are more important than others. The resulting diagram could form the basis of an essay plan.

To what extent did economic modernisation in Germany in the years 1900–1914 heighten existing social tensions?

1. Exceptional economic growth, 1890–1914
2. Creation of new industries
3. Industrialisation of the German economy
4. Urbanisation
5. Improved transport infrastructure
6. Working-class poverty

Heightened existing social tensions   Did not heighten existing social tensions

Political developments

Social and economic change produced greater **polarisation** of German politics.

The left

A growing urban working class led to the expansion of **left-wing** political organisations. By 1900, Germany's trade union movement was the largest in the world and the main left-wing party, the **SPD**, saw their support increase substantially. The growth of the working class and the growth of the left provided a social and political challenge to Germany's conservative elite. The consequences of this for the political system are explored on page 12.

Election results for the SPD 1887–1912

Party	1887**	1890	1893	1898	1903	1907	1912
SPD seats in the Reichstag*	11	35	44	56	81	43	110***
Percentage of the vote (rounded)	0.03%	0.9%	11%	14%	20%	11%	28%

*Out of a total of 397 seats

**Anti-socialist laws that limited the possible representation of the SPD were in place in 1887

***The SPD were now the largest party in the Reichstag

The right

The changing economic and social situation in Germany also caused a rise in **nationalist politics** with elements in the German Conservative Party (DKP) moving in an extremist direction. The parties that represented the new business elite, such as the NLP, became increasingly conservative. Right-wing **pressure groups** sought to protect the social elite from free market policies and also to promote nationalism and colonial and military expansion.

Political parties and pressure groups in the Second Reich

The DKP – German Conservative Party

This party represented *Junkers* and was strong in Prussia. The party often had links with the government. From the 1890s, elements within the DKP became more radical and **anti-Semitic** elements were inserted into the party's constitution.

FKP – Free Conservative Party

Supported by industrialists and landowners, the party had broad geographical support.

NLP – National Liberal Party

Represented bankers and industrialists. Supported economic and political **liberalism** but over time the NLP's political agenda came to be similar to that of the DKP.

The Centre (Zentrum/Z) Party

This party represented German Catholics (around a third of Germans). It consistently received approximately a quarter of votes in Reichstag elections. The party usually worked more with conservative parties, but at times (for example over the budget in 1906) sided with the SPD. Thus the Centre Party often held the **balance of power** in the Reichstag.

The SPD – Social Democratic Party

The SPD theoretically had revolutionary aims. However, the party was mainly moderate and reformist.

The Agrarian League

Formed as a pressure group in 1893 by *Junkers* seeking **protectionist** measures against competition. The League also had a nationalist and anti-Semitic bent. The League had links with the DKP.

The Central Association of German Industrialists

This powerful group called for tariffs to protect German industry from foreign competition. The organisation gave funding to a great many conservative members of the Reichstag.

The Navy League

The Navy League campaigned for German naval expansion. The League was very popular and had a membership of around 1 million.

The German Colonial League and the Pan German League

These two right-wing groups supported German colonial expansion. The Pan German League, whose members in the Reichstag were usually National Liberals, also sought a dominant role for Germany in Europe.

Spot the mistake

Below are a sample Part (a) exam-style question and a paragraph written in answer to this question. Why does this paragraph not get into Level 4? Once you have identified the mistake, rewrite the paragraph so that it displays the qualities of Level 4. The mark scheme on page 117 will help you.

To what extent was the rise in support for the Social Democratic Party a result of Germany's economic modernisation?

One reason for the rise in support of the Social Democratic Party (SPD) was Germany's economic modernisation. For example, Germany experienced a lot of economic growth and the creation of new industries. At the same time, Germany became, for the first time in its history, an industrial economy. This led to urbanisation and poor living standards, which in turn led to class tensions. Therefore, one reason for the rise in support of the SPD was economic modernisation because it led to a rise in class tensions and consequently the popularity of left-wing political parties.

Develop the detail

Below are the sample Part (a) exam-style question and the paragraph written in answer to this question from the activity above. The paragraph contains a limited amount of detail. Annotate the paragraph to add additional detail to the answer.

To what extent was the rise in support for the Social Democratic Party a result of Germany's economic modernisation?

One reason for the rise in support of the Social Democratic Party (SPD) was Germany's economic modernisation. For example, Germany experienced a lot of economic growth and the creation of new industries. At the same time, Germany became, for the first time in its history, an industrial economy. This led to urbanisation and poor living standards, which in turn led to class tensions. Therefore, one reason for the rise in support of the SPD was economic modernisation because it led to a rise in class tensions and consequently the popularity of left-wing political parties.

The Kaiser and his Chancellors

Kaiser Wilhelm II ascended to the throne of Prussia and the German Empire in 1888. The Kaiser sought a dominant role in German politics and moved in 1890 against his powerful Chancellor, Bismarck. Kaiser Wilhelm is often portrayed as an **autocrat** who sought political control and developed aggressive and **militaristic** policies in the years leading up to the First World War.

Kaiser Wilhelm II's childhood

Kaiser Wilhelm was born in 1859, the son of Prince Frederick Wilhelm of Prussia and Victoria, the Princess Royal of Britain. Kaiser Wilhelm was born with a **withered arm**. The Kaiser is considered to have had a difficult childhood: relations between him and his parents were often strained, and he seems to have been troubled by his disability. Some historians have viewed Wilhelm as a **megalomaniac**, psychologically damaged by his childhood.

The 1890s

Historian John Röhl argues that the Kaiser developed a system of autocratic **personal rule** during the 1890s: he appointed ministers who would further his conservative political agenda and sought to control the work of his Chancellors and government. Bismarck's replacement, Caprivi, found the Kaiser interfering and difficult to work with and he attempted to resign five times, before Wilhelm eventually allowed him to in 1894. Caprivi was replaced by the aristocratic and aging Hohenlohe who was largely controlled by the Kaiser and his ministers. In 1896–1897 the Kaiser exercised his powers of **patronage** to remove more **progressive** ministers from the government and replace them with those who shared his conservative vision, such as von Bülow and von Tirpitz.

Chancellor von Bülow, 1900–1909

Requiring a more effective politician to work with the Reichstag in order to get their support for his imperial and military plans, Kaiser Wilhelm appointed Bernhard von Bülow as Chancellor in 1900. Von Bülow outwardly co-operated with the Kaiser, but sometimes succeeded in sidelining or defeating him, for example over the **Tariff Law** of 1902. The Kaiser tried to reassert his authority once again by making a series of ministerial appointments in 1905–1906.

Von Bülow sought to align conservative and **centrist** political forces in Germany through unifying them around foreign policy, a policy known as 'bringing together' or *Sammlungspolitik*. He had some success in building Reichstag support by creating a voting bloc (the 'Bülow Bloc') of all the non-socialist parties. Von Bülow also tried to appease socialist forces in a series of social reforms, such as measures relating to sickness insurance in 1903 and child labour in 1908. However, he faced a serious challenge to his authority from the Reichstag during the budgetary crisis and **Hottentot election** of 1906–1907. In the end, von Bülow resigned, having lost the support of the Kaiser in the aftermath of the *Daily Telegraph* Affair (see page 12).

Chancellor Bethmann Hollweg, 1909–1916

Bethmann's chancellorship illustrates the Reichstag's lack of control over the government. In 1913, following the Zabern Affair (see page 12), Bethmann lost a **vote of no-confidence** in the SPD-dominated Reichstag. However, the Reichstag did not have the constitutional power to force him out of office and therefore he remained Chancellor.

Bethmann had more success with the Army Bill earlier in 1913, where he gained SPD support for army expansion by agreeing to fund it through **progressive taxation**.

Support or challenge?

Below is a sample Part (a) exam-style question which asks how far you agree with a specific statement. Below this is a series of general statements which are relevant to the question. Using your own knowledge and the information on the opposite page decide whether these statements support or challenge the statement in the question and tick the appropriate box.

'The Second Reich was essentially a system of autocratic personal rule by the Kaiser in the period 1900–1914.' How far do you agree with this opinion?

	SUPPORT	CHALLENGE
The Kaiser was the Commander-in-Chief of the Armed Forces.		
The Kaiser could not initiate legislation.		
The Kaiser replaced von Bülow with Bethmann following the *Daily Telegraph* Affair.		
In 1913, Bethmann lost a vote of no-confidence in the Reichstag.		
The SPD became the largest party in the Reichstag in 1912.		
Urbanisation led to a growth in the trade union movement.		
The Reichstag was elected by all men over the age of 25.		
The Reichstag could veto or amend legislation.		

Complete the Venn diagram

Use the information that you have gained so far to add detail to the Venn diagram below. In the non-intersecting areas of the diagram, list the roles of the Kaiser, the Chancellor, and the Reichstag. In the intersecting areas of the diagram, list the tensions between these groups and individuals. These can be general tensions, resulting from the constitution, or specific tensions, resulting from specific events.

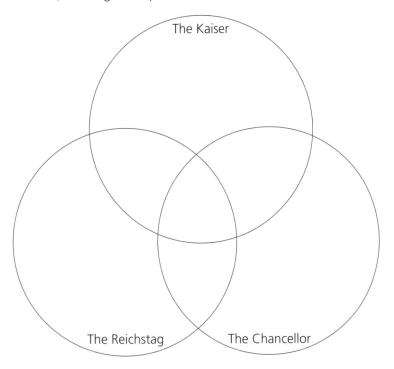

How did the political system work in practice?

Tensions in the German political system

By 1914, the political system did not work very effectively. As the Kaiser appointed the government, they remained permanently conservative, upper class and *Junker*-dominated, while the largest party in the Reichstag was, from 1912, the SPD, which represented the working class. Consequently, governments often struggled to work with the Reichstag. These tensions can be seen in the following events:

The budgetary crisis 1906 and the Hottentot election 1907

In 1906 the SPD and the Centre Party deputies in the Reichstag joined forces to vote against the government's budget, in protest at Germany's colonial policies. The Kaiser consequently used his powers to dissolve the Reichstag and a new election was called in 1907, known as the Hottentot election. Conservative **imperialist** parties emerged strengthened after the election.

This event demonstrated:

■ the Reichstag trying to control the actions of the Kaiser, government and army

■ the tensions between a left-wing Reichstag and a permanently conservative government

■ the power that the Kaiser had to dissolve the Reichstag

■ support from the German public for a brutal imperialist agenda.

The *Daily Telegraph* Affair, 1908

In 1908, conversations that the Kaiser had with a British colonel were published in the *Daily Telegraph*. The Kaiser made various unguarded comments, such as that the British were 'mad, mad as March hares!' for thinking that Germany posed a threat to peace. He implied that German naval build-up was directed at the Japanese. The Kaiser was perceived in Germany as having exceeded his authority in talking to the foreign press in this way. The affair led to wider criticism of the Kaiser in the Reichstag and the press. They criticised his conduct and his dominance

in foreign affairs. The Kaiser eventually agreed to guarantee to the Reichstag that he would not make similar pronouncements in future. Kaiser Wilhelm avoided political interventions following this event but did pressurise von Bülow, whom he felt had been too supportive of the Reichstag, to resign.

This event demonstrated that:

■ the Reichstag and the German press were prepared to criticise the Kaiser

■ the Reichstag could gain concessions from the Kaiser

■ the Kaiser could not always act in an autocratic manner

■ the Kaiser could remove his Chancellors.

The Zabern Affair, 1913

A German soldier based in Zabern, in Alsace, made a derogatory comment about the Alsatian locals. Tensions escalated between the German army and local inhabitants, and matters came to a head when the soldier was acquitted by a military court of injuring a man who had jeered at him. The Kaiser backed the military, while the Reichstag criticised the conduct of the army and of Chancellor Bethmann, eventually passing a vote of no-confidence in him. Scheidemann of the SPD called upon Bethmann to resign but he refused, saying he depended only upon the authority of the Kaiser.

This event demonstrated that:

■ the army operated independently of civil authority in Germany and were accountable to the Kaiser who, by 1913, was very supportive of them

■ the Reichstag were not able to hold the Chancellor to account: the Chancellor only needed the Kaiser's support

■ the Reichstag could be ignored by the Kaiser and the army

■ tensions existed between different parts of the German system, especially between the army and the Reichstag.

Spectrum of significance

Below are a sample Part (a) exam-style question and a list of general points which could be used to answer the question. Use your own knowledge and the information on the opposite page to reach a judgement about the importance of these general points to the question posed. Write numbers on the spectrum below to indicate their relative importance. Having done this, write a brief justification of your placement, explaining why some of these factors are more important than others. The resulting diagram could form the basis of an essay plan.

'The Second Reich became increasingly democratic in the years 1900–1914.' How far do you agree with this opinion?

1. The budgetary crisis, 1906
2. The Hottentot election, 1907
3. The *Daily Telegraph* Affair, 1908

4. The dismissal of von Bülow, 1909
5. The Zabern Affair, 1913
6. The vote of no-confidence in Bethmann, 1913

Democratic   Autocratic

Introducing an argument

Below are a sample Part (a) exam-style question, a list of key points to be made in the essay and a simple introduction and conclusion for the essay. Read the question, the plan and the introduction and conclusion. Rewrite the introduction and conclusion in order to develop an argument.

'The Second Reich was essentially an entrenched autocracy.' How far do you agree with this opinion?

Key points:

- The constitutional role of the Kaiser
- The Kaiser's desire to establish 'personal rule'
- The constitutional role of the Reichstag

- The growth of left-wing influence in the Reichstag
- The impact of constitutional crises, 1906–1913

Introduction

> There is clearly evidence for and against the statement that the Second Reich was essentially an entrenched autocracy. On the one hand, the constitutional role of the Kaiser and the Kaiser's desire to establish 'personal rule' suggest that Germany was indeed an entrenched autocracy. On the other hand, the constitutional role of the Reichstag, the growth of left-wing influence in the Reichstag, and the impact of constitutional crises in the period 1906–1913 suggest that there were democratic checks on the power of the Kaiser.

Conclusion

> There is clearly evidence for and against the statement that the Second Reich was essentially an entrenched autocracy. Overall, the events of 1900–1914 suggest that the Second Reich was more autocratic than it was democratic.

The Second Reich by 1914

Historians debate how the political system of the Second Reich operated and where power lay in this system.

- John Röhl suggests that the Kaiser built an autocratic semi-absolutist system within which his militaristic and conservative agenda was advanced, the Reichstag sidelined and liberal and democratic forces weakened.

- The Second Reich could also be seen as a failing system that was unable to cope with the political and social challenges that a modernising economy had produced. Hans-Ulrich Wehler argued that Germany was dominated by powerful conservative forces, such as the army, that were not democratically accountable.

- Christopher Clark argues that the system was too fluid and the Kaiser too erratic for personal rule by Wilhelm to have been possible. Clark is more positive than Röhl or Wehler about the strength of liberal elements in Germany at this time.

- Geoff Eley and David Blackburn have emphasised the scale and range of political participation in the Second Reich: they focus upon the impact of **politics from below** rather than **politics from above**.

Entrenched autocracy, elite dominance or a growing democracy?

Evidence that Germany was an autocracy

- The Kaiser had the power to appoint the Chancellor and ministers and the power to dissolve the Reichstag. The Kaiser shaped the composition of the government 1896–1897 and 1905–1906, and dissolved the Reichstag in 1906. He also forced von Bülow to resign after the *Daily Telegraph* Affair.

- The Chancellor and ministers were not accountable to the Reichstag. Bethmann lost a vote of no-confidence in the Reichstag and remained as Chancellor.

- The army was only accountable to the Kaiser and so was not affected by the Reichstag's criticisms following the Zabern Affair in 1913.

- The country followed the Kaiser's political agenda, for example in **Weltpolitik** (see page 24).

Evidence that Germany was dominated by a conservative elite

- The agenda of the conservative elite was followed in naval, militaristic and colonial expansion. This was reflected in colonial policies and in the Naval Bill of 1906.

- Conservative pressure groups like the Agrarian League and the Central Association of German Industrialists successfully **lobbied** for increased agricultural tariffs in 1902.

- The power of the Bundesrat meant that the government was dominated by conservatives.

- A conservative Prussian elite dominated the state in the army, judiciary, civil service and government.

Evidence of democracy and liberalism in Germany

- The Reichstag was democratic in the sense that all classes of men had the vote.

- The Reichstag was able to reject legislation and did so in 1906 when they rejected colonial policy.

- The Reichstag were increasingly assertive, as can be seen from their stance on the 1906 budget, their criticisms of the Kaiser in the wake of the *Daily Telegraph* Affair in 1908 and their censure of Bethmann in 1913.

- The ruling elite had to respond to pressure from below (from left-wing political movements and the working classes) for social reform.

- The press criticised the Kaiser, for example after the *Daily Telegraph* affair.

- Political participation was high: the trade union movement was large, pressure groups influential and women participated in political movements despite not having the vote.

- There was a **plurality** of interests in the state: Catholics had the Centre Party; workers the SPD; farmers the Agrarian League.

RAG – Rate the timeline

Below are a sample Part (a) exam-style question and a timeline. Read the question, study the timeline and, using three coloured pens, put a Red, Amber or Green star next to the events to show:

Red: Events and policies that have no relevance to the question
Amber: Events and policies that have some significance to the question
Green: Events and policies that are directly relevant to the question

1) To what extent was the Second Reich dominated politically and socially by the German elites in the period 1900–1914?

Now repeat the activity with the following question:

2) 'The Second Reich was characterised by fundamental economic and political divisions in the period 1900–1914.' How far do you agree with this opinion?

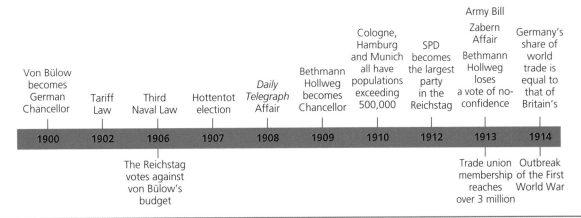

Developing an argument

Below are a sample Part (a) exam-style question, a list of key points to be made in the essay and a paragraph from the essay. Read the question, the plan and the sample paragraph. Rewrite the paragraph in order to develop an argument. Your paragraph should explain why the factor discussed in the paragraph is either the most significant factor or less significant than another factor.

To what extent was the Kaiser the most powerful figure in the Second Reich in the period 1900–1914?

Key points:

- The Kaiser
- The army
- The Reichstag
- The *Junkers*
- The Chancellor

Sample paragraph

> The Chancellor clearly had significant power within the Second Reich. Constitutionally, the Chancellor was responsible for presenting legislation to the Reichstag. Additionally, the Chancellor was not democratically accountable to the German people, in the sense that he could not be dismissed by the Reichstag. This was obvious in 1913, when Bethmann lost a vote of no-confidence following the Zabern Affair, but retained his position as he still enjoyed the support of the Kaiser. The budgetary crisis of 1906 is another example of the Chancellor's power. During the crisis, the SPD and the Centre Party joined forces to defeat von Bülow's budget. Nonetheless, with the support of the Kaiser, the Chancellor fought and won the 1907 Hottentot election, following which he was able to reassert his control over the government. In this way, the Chancellor clearly had a great deal of power within the Second Reich as he was unaccountable to the German people and the Reichstag.

The impact of the First World War on Germany

Initially the war appeared to have united Germans but, as the strain of fighting heightened, tensions and disagreements resurfaced.

The economic impact of the war

Fighting the war was an enormous economic strain. Only 16 per cent of the £8.4 million cost of the war was met by taxation: **war bonds** were also used and money printed. Printing money led to **inflation**: the **mark** declined in value by 75 per cent between 1913 and 1918. The KRA, War Raw Materials Department, had some success in supplying the German army but German agriculture was not **mobilised** effectively and there were food shortages.

The social impact of the war

The impact of the war was often severe. Two million soldiers were killed and 6.3 million were injured. With inflation and tight controls on wages, living standards fell by 20–30 per cent. Shortages caused by the war effort and by the British blockade of German ports led to the 'Turnip winter' of 1917 when turnips were the main food available. Food and fuel shortages caused misery, and even starvation, and exacerbated the impact of the **Spanish flu pandemic** in 1918.

The political impact of the war

Initial unity

At the start of the war, Germany appeared politically unified: a **Burgfriede**, or political truce, was declared and the Kaiser, addressing the Reichstag, announced that 'I know no parties anymore, I know only Germans'. However, this situation did not last: the view of the left that only **defensive** war was justified was not compatible with the aim of many on the right for a war of expansion and conquest (a **Siegfriede**).

Growing disunity

By 1917, 42 SPD deputies had broken away to form the anti-war and radical socialist **USPD**. Mounting concern about the war led to a Reichstag vote, the 'peace resolution', which urged the government to try to negotiate a peace settlement. The left and the centre won the vote by 212 to 126.

The war saw the formation of the communist **Spartacist League** who agitated for **social revolution** and an end to the war. Discontent among German workers rose from 1916, as workers were prevented from freely changing jobs under the terms of the Auxiliary Service Law of December 1916. There was, by 1918, widespread discontent and in January 1918 there were significant strikes in many areas, such as one in Berlin for five days involving half a million workers. The war had started by unifying the political scene but, by 1918, political polarisation was greater than it had been before the conflict.

The 'silent dictatorship'

During the war, the government became increasingly authoritarian and militaristic. The Kaiser was sidelined by the military and, by 1916, Supreme Commanders Generals Hindenburg and Ludendorff were essentially in charge of the country, running what has been characterised as a 'silent dictatorship'. An isolated Bethmann was forced out of office by the Generals and Georg Michaelis and then Georg von Hertling became Chancellors. Michaelis and von Hertling were regarded as puppets of Ludendorff and Hindenburg. Military government exacerbated political and social tensions.

The impact of impending defeat

Germany's impending defeat came as a great shock to many Germans. This contributed to the outbreak of the revolution and the acceptance of the '**stab in the back myth**'.

Simple essay style

Below is a sample Part (a) exam-style question. Use your own knowledge and the information on the opposite page to produce a plan for this question. Choose four general points and provide three pieces of specific information to support each general point. Once you have planned your essay, write the introduction and conclusion for the essay. The introduction should list the points to be discussed in the essay. The conclusion should summarise the key points and justify which point was the most important.

> To what extent did the First World War increase Germany's existing political divisions?

Introducing an argument

Below are a sample Part (a) exam-style question, a list of key points to be made in the essay, and a simple introduction and conclusion for the essay. Read the question, the plan, and the introduction and conclusion. Rewrite the introduction and conclusion in order to develop an argument.

> To what extent did increasing political divisions represent the main consequence of the First World War for Germany?

Key points:

- Increasing political divisions
- Economic changes
- Social changes
- Initial unity
- Growing disunity
- 'Silent dictatorship'

Introduction

> The First World War had a substantial impact on Germany. Outcomes included increasing political divisions, economic changes, social changes, initial unity, growing disunity, and the creation of the 'silent dictatorship'.

Conclusion

> The First World War had many impacts on Germany. The most important outcome was increasing political divisions. This was more significant than all of the other factors.

The German Revolution, 1918–1919

The Second Reich began to collapse in the final weeks of the war. The country shifted towards democracy and to some extent saw a social revolution with a weakening of aristocratic power. However, the German revolution was not a total revolution as many elements of the old regime remained.

The German Revolution, 1918–1919

Key event	Description	A democratic revolution	A social revolution?
The revolution from above 29 September – 3 October 1918	Realising that defeat was certain, the Generals advised Kaiser Wilhelm to negotiate an **armistice** and form a new civilian government containing members of the Reichstag. On 3 October, liberal Prince Max of Baden formed a new government containing liberal and socialist members of the Reichstag.	• Authoritarian military rule was at an end. • Reichstag deputies formed part of the government. • The new government included members of the largest party in the Reichstag, the SPD. • The new government and the army and navy were now accountable to the democratic Reichstag.	• The government was no longer solely aristocrats and *Junkers* but now contained the middle class and workers too. • The government was now accountable to the Reichstag, which represented the middle class and working class.
The revolution from below 31 October – 8 November 1918	As realisation of impending defeat spread, sailors in Kiel mutinied against an order to put to sea. The mutiny soon spread to other ports and many other parts of Germany. **Soviets** sprang up across the country and there were riots and disturbances in the Ruhr, Berlin, Cologne, Dresden, Leipzig and Stuttgart. The government had lost control.	• Many ordinary Germans were involved in the disturbances.	• The sailors and workers' soviets represented a new and radical form of political organisation in Germany which saw power passed to the working class.
The abdication of the Kaiser and the declaration of a republic 9 November 1918	Fearing a violent revolution and with the SPD calling for a republic, Hindenburg advised the Kaiser to abdicate. The Kaiser fled to Holland: the Second Reich was at an end and a government of SPD and USPD members was formed. Ebert of the SPD was a dominant member.	• The unelected, hereditary monarch was gone, and elected politicians replaced him in political leadership in Germany. • The dominant figure in government, Ebert, was the leader of the largest party in the Reichstag.	• The man at the pinnacle of the class system, Kaiser Wilhelm II, was removed and politicians of working-class origin such as Ebert replaced him. • The government was formed of the representatives of the working class rather than aristocrats.
Armistice 11 November 1918	The new government signed an armistice agreement with the **Allies**.		
The revolution contained 10 November 1918 – January 1919	Ebert was anti-communist and determined to prevent the German revolution becoming a civil war. He thus did a deal with the army to gain their support (the **Ebert–Groener Pact**) and called for early democratic elections.	• Elections were held in January 1919 on the basis of **universal suffrage**. • The elections produced a constituent assembly which wrote the new German constitution.	• The *Junker* class remained dominant in the judiciary and civil service and the army remained unreformed. • Soviets did not get power.

The flaw in the argument
(a)

Below are a sample Part (a) exam-style question and a paragraph written in answer to this question. The paragraph contains an argument, but there is a flaw in this argument. Use your knowledge of the topic to identify the flaw in the argument.

To what extent was Germany's military defeat in the First World War the main cause of the fall of the Second Reich?

> The most significant factor in the fall of the Second Reich was the power of the Kaiser. The Kaiser established a personal dictatorship which sidelined the liberal and democratic elements of the constitution. For example, the Kaiser used his power to appoint Chancellors who would pursue policies that he supported. In 1900, he appointed Chancellor von Bülow who, with the exception of the Tariff Law of 1902, co-operated with the Kaiser. When von Bülow failed to co-operate with the Kaiser in the Daily Telegraph affair of 1908, the Kaiser replaced him with Bethmann. The Kaiser also ignored popular opinion and supported Bethmann against a vote of no-confidence in 1913, following the Zabern Affair. The Kaiser's power was the main reason for the fall of the Second Reich because, by 1918, he was the most powerful man in Germany, but he did not enjoy the support of the German people.

Recommended reading

Below is a list of suggested further reading on this topic.

- *From Kaiser to Führer: Germany 1900–1945*, Chapters 1–2, Geoff Layton (2009)
- *Kaiser Willhelm II: A Life in Power*, Chapter 4, Christopher Clark (2009)
- *Germany from Reich to Republic, 1871–1918: Politics, Hierarchy and Elites*, Chapters 5 and 7, Matthew S Seligmann and Roderick R McLean (2000)

Exam focus

Below is a sample A grade Part (a) essay. Read it and the examiner comments around it.

To what extent was the Second Reich an entrenched autocracy in the years 1900–1914?

This is a focused introduction that differentiates between 'autocracy' and 'entrenched autocracy'. Rather than defining terms explicitly, the candidate assures the examiner they understand them by the confidence with which they construct an argument.

The Second Reich was certainly an autocracy in the years 1900–1914 in the sense that the Bismarckian constitution gave the Kaiser a great deal of power that was unchecked by the German people. However, the autocracy was not entrenched as there was a series of constitutional crises which showed that the Kaiser's power was not absolute. Moreover, the Daily Telegraph Affair and the Hottentot election of 1907 showed that the Kaiser was forced to collaborate with the democratic aspects of the constitution. Nonetheless, in areas where the Reichstag had no constitutional authority, the Kaiser proved more difficult to control and continued to act as an autocrat.

This paragraph shows detailed knowledge of the constitution of the Second Reich and the powers of the Kaiser.

The constitution of the Second Reich gave the Kaiser near-autocratic powers. The constitution recognised the Kaiser as the sovereign of the Second Reich, Commander-in-Chief of the army, and the most significant figure in the formulation of German foreign policy. In addition to these powers, the Kaiser had the right to dissolve the Reichstag and to appoint the Chancellor. In all of these areas, the Kaiser's power was supreme and required no democratic authorisation. In practice, the Kaiser was willing to use his power to shape government. For example, in 1900, he appointed von Bülow as Chancellor, hoping that he could exercise power over his decisions. When von Bülow asserted his own authority in the aftermath of the Daily Telegraph affair, he was forced to resign, as he had lost the support of the Kaiser. There were therefore strong autocratic elements within the constitution, because the Kaiser played a large role in government and was not accountable to the people.

Having dealt with the Kaiser's constitutional power, this paragraph deals with the Kaiser's power in practice. Again, the paragraph distinguishes between 'autocracy' and 'entrenched autocracy'.

Nonetheless, there was a series of crises which showed the limits of the Kaiser's autocratic power. For example, the budgetary crisis of 1906 indicates that there were obstacles to the Kaiser's 'personal rule'. In 1906, the SPD and the Centre Party joined forces in the Reichstag to oppose the brutal imperialist policies of the Kaiser's government. The SPD and the Centre Party vetoed the government's budget in protest at the imperialist policies of the Kaiser's government. Additionally, the Daily Telegraph Affair of 1908 resulted in new limits to the Kaiser's power. Following an indiscreet interview about foreign policy, published in the Daily Telegraph, the Kaiser was forced to assure the Reichstag that he would never act in this way again. In essence, the Kaiser had capitulated to public pressure, the pressure of the Reichstag, and pressure from von Bülow, and agreed to limit his own power in an area in which the constitution stated he was supreme. Clearly, there were limits to the Kaiser's autocratic power and the fact that the Kaiser was forced to surrender his freedom of action in foreign policy in 1908 indicates that autocracy was not entrenched, because there was opportunity for reform within the existing constitution.

In spite of the successful limitation of the Kaiser's power following the Daily Telegraph Affair, the Reichstag was unable to constrain the Kaiser following the Zabern Affair of 1913. This indicates that, in certain areas, the Second Reich was very difficult to reform, suggesting that the Kaiser's powers were entrenched. In 1913, a German soldier based in Zabern was offensive to some of the ethnically French local people. A fight broke out and yet a military court acquitted the soldier. The SPD criticised the affair and won a vote of no-confidence in the Chancellor and the Kaiser's government. However, the Kaiser refused to back down, asserting his constitutional role as Commander-in-Chief and his constitutional right to appoint the Chancellor. Consequently, the government survived the vote of no-confidence. The Zabern Affair was evidence that reforming the Second Reich could be extremely difficult because reform depended on the co-operation of the Kaiser.

The complexity of the nature of the Second Reich is best illustrated by the Hottentot election of 1907, in which the Kaiser reasserted his power through a democratic election. Following his government's budgetary defeat in the Reichstag, the Kaiser used his constitutional power to dissolve the Reichstag and call a new election. The Kaiser and conservative parties appealed to the popular desire to extend the German empire. Consequently, the public voted in favour of imperialist parties and the Kaiser was able to reassert his dominance over the government. The Hottentot election demonstrates that, in spite of the Kaiser's constitutional power, the power of the Reichstag to veto important government legislation could force the Kaiser to work within the democratic system. In this sense, the Hottentot election indicates that Germany was in fact a popular autocracy, in which the Kaiser was forced to collaborate with democratic institutions, such as elections, rather than an entrenched autocracy in which the Kaiser could do as he pleased.

In conclusion, the Second Reich was an autocracy with some democratic features. It was not a fully entrenched autocracy as, although the Kaiser had a large degree of autocratic power, the Reichstag retained an important right to veto the government's proposals. As a result, the Reichstag was able to curb the Kaiser's power following the Daily Telegraph Affair, and to place a temporary halt on the Kaiser's foreign policy in 1906. However, in areas such as the appointment of the Chancellor, and control of the military, where the Reichstag had no constitutional power, the Kaiser was able to exercise a large degree of autocratic power.

This paragraph demonstrates a nuanced understanding of the Kaiser's constitutional power by contrasting the power of the Kaiser and the power of the Reichstag over the military.

This paragraph uses the example of the Hottentot election to demonstrate the complexities of the government of the Second Reich.

The conclusion pulls together the argument that was initiated in the introduction and developed throughout the essay. In this sense, the essay presents a consistent argument.

30/30

This is a Level 5 essay due to the fact that it has a clear argument that is sustained throughout the essay. This argument contrasts the democratic and autocratic aspects of the constitution, and arrives at a judgement by arguing that successful reforms of the Kaiser's power meant that his autocracy was not fully entrenched.

Section 2: To what extent was Germany responsible for the outbreak of the First World War?

The historical debate

In the aftermath of the First World War the victorious countries seemed in no doubt about who had caused the war: Germany and Germany's **allies**. The **Treaty of Versailles** included a 'war guilt clause' which compelled Germany to accept responsibility for the war. Following the Second World War, however, and in the context of reconciliation between France and Germany, the historical consensus was that the First World War had been a collective European failure. It was argued that the European diplomatic system of opposing alliances and competition over empires and weapons had caused countries to move towards conflict: no single country could be singled out for particular blame.

The Fischer Thesis

This historical consensus was challenged in 1961 by German historian Fritz Fischer who argued in his book, *Germany's Aims in the First World War*, that in the years prior to the First World War Germany had a plan for European domination which led to the pursuit of an aggressive foreign policy and ultimately war. Fischer developed his arguments in his 1969 *War of Illusions*. His contentions caused consternation, particularly in German historical circles, and a debate has continued ever since about the extent of German culpability for the First World War.

Arguments that Germany was responsible

Some of the arguments that have been made to support the idea that Germany was responsible for starting the war include the following:

- Under Kaiser Wilhelm II's leadership, Germany pursued European **hegemony** (dominance).
- Before the First World War, Germany's foreign policy was nationalistic and **militaristic**.

- Germany planned to have a major European war in order to gain hegemony in Europe.
- Germany antagonised other **Great Powers** in Europe in the years leading up to the war and followed a course of confrontation with Russia, France and Britain.
- Germany took decisions in the summer of 1914, following the death of Archduke Franz Ferdinand (see page 28), that led to war.

Arguments that Germany was not entirely responsible

Others have countered with the following:

- There is no clear evidence that Germany had a long-term plan of aggression in relation to the First World War: they just planned for the *possibility* of a war. It could be argued that Germany felt that in the Entente powers they faced an aggressive and hostile coalition.
- Other European powers participated in events that caused conflict in the years leading to the First World War.
- All European Great Powers were part of an alliance system that created tensions between nations in Europe before the war.
- Britain, France, Russia and Germany contributed to the build-up of weapons before the First World War.
- The crisis following the murder of Franz Ferdinand that led to war in the summer of 1914 was not started by Germany and nor was Germany the only power to make decisions in July 1914 that caused the conflict to escalate.

Linking sources

Below are a sample Part (b) exam-style question and the three sources referred to in the question. In one colour, draw links between the sources to show ways in which they agree about German responsibility for the outbreak of war in 1914. In another colour, draw links between the sources to show ways in which they disagree.

Use Sources 1, 2 and 3 and your own knowledge.

To what extent do you agree with the view that 'German leaders must bear a substantial share of the historical responsibility for the outbreak of a general war in 1914'?

SOURCE 1

(From Niall Ferguson in The War of the World, *published 2006)*

Historians have, on the whole, tended to portray the years before the outbreak of the First World War as a time of mounting tension and escalating crises. War, they have claimed, did not burst on to the scene in the summer of 1914; rather, it approached over a period of years, even decades. European societies, it is now widely agreed, were ready for war long before war came.

The reality is that the First World War was a shock, not a long-anticipated crisis. Only retrospectively did men decide that they had seen it coming all along.

SOURCE 2

(From Fritz Fischer in Germany's Aims in the First World War, *published 1967)*

Given the tenseness of the world situation in 1914 – a condition for which Germany's world policy, which had already led to three dangerous crises (those of 1905, 1908 and 1911), was in no small measure responsible – any limited or local war in Europe directly involving one great power must inevitably carry with it the imminent danger of a general war. As Germany willed and coveted the Austro-Serbian war and, in her confidence in her military superiority, deliberately faced the risk of a conflict with Russia and France, her leaders must bear a substantial share of the historical responsibility for the outbreak of general war in 1914.

SOURCE 3

(From James Joll and Gordon Martell in The Origins of the First World War, *published 2007)*

Throughout [July 1914] the German leaders repeated on several occasions their support for Austria–Hungary and pressed on the Austrians the advantages of rapid action. The Austrian ambassador in Berlin reported that government circles there believed that the moment was a favourable one even in the case of Russian intervention, since the Russians were not yet fully prepared militarily and not nearly as strong as they were likely to be in a few years. While the discussions about the precise terms of the ultimatum were going on in Vienna, the allies in Berlin were repeatedly urging the need for action and leaving their own willingness to risk war in no doubt, and they even showed some anxiety at the delay in dispatching the ultimatum.

Did Germany have a long-term plan for European hegemony?

The Fischer Thesis

Fischer, and others who support his view such as John Röhl, writing in Britain in the 1990s, advance a number of different pieces of evidence to support the **thesis** that Germany sought European dominance and was to blame for the First World War.

Weltpolitik

From the 1890s, Germany followed a policy of ***Weltpolitik*** (world politics) which entailed seeking colonial expansion and a more dominant position in Europe and the world. Germany built up its military might, particularly through naval expansion, and acquired imperial possessions in Africa. From 1896, the Kaiser shaped his government to include ministers and Chancellors (such as von Bülow) who shared his vision. *Weltpolitik* can be interpreted as confrontational as it challenged the status of other European powers. For many German nationalists, *Weltpolitik* was also about German expansion into Eastern Europe.

The Schlieffen Plan 1905

The Schlieffen Plan (see page 28) can be interpreted as a plan for a war of aggression, as it entailed potentially unprovoked German attacks on France and Belgium.

The War Council 1912

At a meeting of the Kaiser and military leaders in 1912, the possibility of a future war with Russia was discussed and plans were made to prepare the German public for such an eventuality. The Kaiser and Field Marshall von Moltke agitated for war and armaments development. For Fischer, the War Council indicates that the Kaiser and his closest military advisors were planning for war in the east from 1912.

The September Programme 1914

The September Programme, written by German Chancellor Bethmann Hollweg, was produced in the early days of the war and outlined Germany's war aims. It contained a clear indication that Germany sought to subordinate France, and also far-reaching plans for German domination in Eastern Europe, including the **annexation** of large amounts of territory with a German **sphere of influence** that stretched all the way to the Ukraine.

Criticisms of Fischer's arguments

However, a number of criticisms can be made of Fischer's use of the evidence:

- The Schlieffen Plan could be regarded as a plan for the *possibility* of a war on two **fronts** rather than a plan to *start* a war on two fronts.
- Fischer may have placed too much weight on the War Council meeting: it was not attended by Chancellor Bethmann Hollweg and little action occurred in response to the meeting.
- The War Council meeting was a response to Britain's declaration that they would support France unconditionally in the event of a war. The War Council may reflect German fears of **encirclement** rather than an aggressive desire for war.
- The September Programme was written only after war had commenced and so cannot necessarily be taken as a clear indication of a plan of aggression and domination that predated the war.

Add own knowledge

Below are a sample Part (b) exam-style question and the three sources referred to in the question. In one colour, draw links between the sources to show ways in which they agree about the importance of *Weltpolitik* as a cause of the First World War. In another colour, draw links between the sources to show ways in which they disagree. Around the edge of the sources, write relevant own knowledge. Again, draw links to show the ways in which this agrees and disagrees with the sources.

Use Sources 1, 2 and 3 and your own knowledge.

To what extent do you agree with the view that '*Weltpolitik* made war inevitable' by August 1914?

SOURCE 1

(From Wilhelm Deist et al. *in* The Kaiser, *published 2003)*

A significant factor of any discussion of the Kaiser's role in the outbreak of the First World War is the 'war council' of 8 December 1912. The Kaiser, impressed by the diplomatic tensions caused by the First Balkan War discussed with his military entourage the necessity of preparations for a major war which was predicted in 1914. The importance of this council remains controversial. Some historians argue that the Kaiser and his entourage agreed that a war was to start in 1914. But the majority believe that the major source which reports on this event, the diary of Admiral von Müller, is right: 'The result of this conversation was more or less zero.' Either way, it has still not proved possible to draw a continuous line from 1912 to the actual outbreak of the war, and thus to establish a connection.

SOURCE 2

(From Imanuel Geiss in Origins of the First World War, *published 1972)*

The events of July and early August 1914 cannot be properly understood without a knowledge of the historical background provided by the preceding decades of Imperialism. On the other hand, that background alone is not sufficient to explain the outbreak of the First World War. Two general historical factors proved to be decisive, and both were fused by a third to produce the explosion known as the First World War. Imperialism, with Wilhelmine *Weltpolitik* as its specifically German version, provided the general framework and the basic tensions: the principle of national self-determination constituted, with its revolutionary potential, a permanent but latent threat to the old dynastic empires and built-up tensions in south-east Europe. The determination of the German Empire – then the most powerful conservative force in the world after Tsarist Russia – to uphold the conservative and monarchic principles by any means by the rising flood of democracy, plus its *Weltpolitik* made war inevitable.

SOURCE 3

(From Annika Mombauer in The Origins of the First World War, *published 2002)*

To Fischer, the 'September-Programme' was a 'blueprint' for world power. 'It was an expression of Germany striving for European hegemony, the first step toward "world domination"', as he summed up in a later publication.

To Fischer's opponents, this claim was unconvincing. They argued that a memorandum written in early September 1914, at a time when Germany was fighting a successful campaign on all fronts, could not serve as evidence for *prewar* aims. Until that date, German troops had been fighting the war on two fronts with great success, and it is likely that the political decision-makers considered an early victory against at least one of Germany's enemies to be imminent.

Did Germany destabilise peace in Europe before 1914?

Another way of looking at the question of whether Germany was responsible for causing the First World War is to examine German actions that contributed to the destabilisation of European peace before 1914.

Antagonising Russia

Bismarck had sought peace with Russia and so had established the Reinsurance Treaty in which Russia and Germany agreed not to attack each other. In 1890, Kaiser Wilhelm II allowed this treaty to lapse and began to seek closer relations with the **Austro-Hungarian Empire**.

In 1908, during the Bosnian crisis, Germany's support for Austrian annexation of Bosnia antagonised Russia, who had demanded an international conference on the issue.

> ### The Bosnian Crisis, 1908
>
> The decline of the power of the **Ottoman Empire** in the Balkans led to instability in the region. From 1878, Serbia was recognised as independent and the Austrian Empire had informal control over Bosnia and Herzegovina. Serbia regarded the Austrians as **imperialists** and, when in 1908 the Austrians formally annexed Bosnia and Herzegovina into the Austrian Empire, the Serbs and their allies, Russia, were outraged. In 1909, Austria pressured Serbia and Russia to accept the annexation by threatening war with Serbia. In Germany, von Bülow's government supported Austria's action and promised military assistance against Serbia.

Antagonising France

Relations between France and Germany were tense throughout the existence of the Second Reich. Germany's involvement in French colonial problems in Morocco in the early part of the twentieth century added to the strain and increased French and British suspicions about Germany:

The First Moroccan Crisis, 1905–6

Kaiser Wilhelm II made a speech in Tangier in Morocco demanding an international conference on France's role in Morocco, which the French were developing as a colony. The Kaiser hoped to isolate France and protect German economic interests in Morocco. At the subsequent conference in Algeciras all countries present accepted French influence in the area except for Germany and Austria–Hungary.

The Second Moroccan Crisis, 1911

Following French suppression of an anti-French uprising in Fez in Morocco, Germany argued that France had exceeded their rights in Morocco and Kaiser Wilhelm II ordered a gunboat, the *Panther*, to be moored off the Moroccan port of Agadir as a threat to France and an indication of support for the rebels. Britain and France regarded German actions as aggressive. Eventually, Germany was given the right to control parts of the Congo in return for accepting French influence in Morocco.

Antagonising Britain

British and German relations were strained by German support for the Boers during the **Boer War 1899–1902**. German naval expansion also caused tensions. The Second Naval Law in 1900 increased the size of the German navy to 38 battleships and further expansion occurred in 1906, 1908 and 1912. The British introduced a new and more manoeuvrable form of warship, the dreadnought, in 1906. The British regarded naval supremacy as crucial to British security and status and were concerned to maintain the principle that the British navy should be at least equal to the size of the combined forces of the next two naval powers. In 1912, Britain tried to negotiate with Germany to limit their naval expansion, but to no avail.

Summarise the interpretation   ⓐ

Below are a sample Part (b) exam-style question and the three sources referred to in the question. Each source offers an interpretation of the issue raised by the question. Next to each source, summarise the interpretation offered by the source.

Use Sources 1, 2 and 3 and your own knowledge.

To what extent do you agree with the view that the First World War was the result of German aggression?

SOURCE 1

(From John Charmley in Splendid Isolation, *published 1999)*

It was the decision to occupy Boznia and Herzegovina in 1908 which, far more than any Anglo-German antagonism, led the way to the confrontation of 1914. It marked a new willingness by the Austrians to use force to deny territory to the Pan-Serbian agitators in Belgrade, which showed the increasing influence of the Austrian Chief of the General Staff, Field-Marshall Franz Conrad Von Hotzendorff, who advocated a forceful solution to the problems which beset the Austrian monarchy. It also marked a new, almost reckless style of diplomacy, the success of which inculcated lessons which would be remembered in 1914. The Bosnian crisis brought Europe to the verge of war for the first time since the 1870s.

SOURCE 2

(From LCF Turner in Origins of the First World War, *published 1970)*

The situation in 1910 presented grave problems but was not beyond control. A.J.P. Taylor has remarked that 'No war is inevitable until it breaks out' and, even if this comment is of dubious validity for 1914, it certainly applies to the period between the end of the Bosnian crisis in March 1909 and the dispatch of the gunboat *Panther* to Agadir in 1911. Although there had been a serious deterioration in international relations since 1905, it would be difficult to argue that the first Moroccan and Bosnian crises had fatally prejudiced the maintenance of European peace. Nevertheless these ominous tests of strength had revealed very disquieting tendencies in German policy.

SOURCE 3

(From Ruth Beatrice Henig in The Origins of the First World War, *published 1993)*

The picture of reduced tensions and of increasing stability amongst Europe's great powers [in 1914] was illusory. It masked great underlying problems and increasing pessimism on the part of many European leaders about developments which they believed were undermining their countries' position and great power status. Since 1900, Europe had been wracked by a series of crises, each of which had brought her great powers closer to war. These crises were provoked by a number of serious issues which were causing mounting friction amongst the powers and which, by 1914, in the opinion of many European statesmen, were becoming insoluble by means other than resort to war.

Did German actions in the summer of 1914 cause war in Europe?

Revised

A further way of looking at German culpability for the First World War is to examine the actions that Germany took in the weeks leading to war.

On 28 June 1914, the heir to the Austrian throne, Archduke Franz Ferdinand, was murdered by Bosnian associates of the Serbian nationalist Black Hand organisation. Austria blamed Serbia for the assassination and a crisis developed that ultimately led to world war.

The July Crisis and the 'Blank Cheque'

- On 5–6 July, encouraged by Generals Ludendorff and Hindenburg, Kaiser Wilhelm II and Chancellor Bethmann Hollweg gave their full support to the Austrians in pursuing a tough line against Serbia, despite the fact that there was no clear evidence that the Serbian government was involved in the assassination.
- Bethmann Hollweg urged the Austrians to take swift military action against the Serbians, and offered whatever financial and military assistance the Austrians required.
- The unconditional German support for the Austrians has been termed the '**Blank Cheque**' and it made armed conflict more likely.
- The Austrians subsequently issued an ultimatum to the Serbians and when one of their ten demands was not met, declared war on Serbia.
- Support for Austria in a local war did not necessarily mean that Germany sought a major European conflict, however, although Bethmann Hollweg certainly seems to have considered the possibility that this would occur, and Generals Ludendorff and Hindenburg were interested in using the conflict to create a war with Russia and gain territory at Russia's expense.

The declaration of war on Russia

On 28 July, Austria declared war on Serbia and in response Russia, who was allied with Serbia and concerned to prevent Austria expanding in the Balkan region, began to **mobilise** her army. On 31 July, Germany declared war on Russia.

The Schlieffen Plan and the invasion of Belgium and France

Despite the conflict only being on the **Eastern Front**, the German political and military elite decided to enact the Schlieffen Plan, as war with Russia might have meant war with France. Germany demanded that Belgium allow German troops to cross their territory and on 3 August 1914 declared war on France. When Belgium refused, Germany launched an invasion of Belgium on 4 August and Britain, who had an alliance with Belgium, declared war on Germany.

The Schlieffen Plan

The Schlieffen Plan was a plan to prevent the possibility of Germany engaging in a war on two fronts: that is, fighting a war simultaneously against France and Russia. The plan assumed that, in the event of war with France and Russia, the size of the Russian army and inefficiency of Russian infrastructure would mean that it would take Russia six weeks to be fully mobilised and ready for war. The plan envisaged the German army using this six-week period to quickly attack and defeat France, and then turn their attention to fighting Russia. In order to make such a quick victory feasible, the Schlieffen Plan entailed Germany invading France via Belgium, as the French border with Belgium was not properly defended and the terrain through Belgium and north-eastern France was fairly flat and easy to cross.

Contrasting interpretations

Below are three sources offering interpretations regarding Germany's responsibility for the outbreak of the First World War. Identify the interpretation offered in each source and complete the table below, indicating how far the sources agree with each other, and explaining your answer.

	Extent of agreement	Justification
Sources 1 and 2		
Sources 1 and 3		
Sources 2 and 3		

SOURCE 1

(From AJP Taylor in War by Time-table, *published 1969)*

When cut down to essentials, the sole cause for the outbreak of war in 1914 was the Schlieffen Plan – product of the belief in speed and the offensive. Diplomacy functioned until the German demand that France and Russia should not mobilise. No power could have accepted such a demand in the circumstances of the age. Yet the Germans had no deliberate aim of subverting the liberties of Europe. No one had time for a deliberate aim or time to think. All were trapped by the ingenuity of their military preparations, the Germans most of all. In every country, the peoples imagined that they were being called to a defensive war, and in a sense they were right. Since every general staff believed that attack was the only form of defence, every defensive operation appeared as an attack to someone else.

SOURCE 2

(From John Horne in A Companion to World War I, *published 2012)*

It is beyond doubt that the German government bears the most immediate responsibility for the outbreak of the war in August 1914. It issued a blank cheque for Austria–Hungary to attack Serbia, guaranteeing German support even if it meant war with Russia. This shows that the German military and political leadership intended to challenge the Franco-Russian alliance even at the price of a European war, and that for many such a war was precisely the desired goal, as a means of settling the Russian 'threat' and breaking Germany's 'encirclement'.

SOURCE 3

(From DCB Lieven in Russia and the Origins of the First World War, *published 1983)*

How important was the general mobilisation of the Russian army on the 31 July? At first glance it would seem to have been crucial since Russia's move was answered immediately by Germany's mobilisation and within two days by the outbreak of war. Even without the Russian mobilisation there is, however, every reason to doubt whether by 30 July a European conflict could have been avoided since, as Russian diplomats stressed, by then Austria and Germany had gone too far to retreat without serious damage to their prestige and to the stability of their alliance. Study of the July Crisis, from the Russian standpoint indeed, confirms the now generally accepted view that the major immediate responsibility for the outbreak of the war rested unequivocally on the German government.

The actions of others and the European system

One criticism of the Fischer thesis is that it focuses too much on German actions and exaggerates German responsibility. Other countries were also involved in decisions and actions that caused tensions and led to war, and it could be argued that Germany acted as they felt that in the Entente, they faced an aggressive coalition.

The actions of others

- Britain participated in the naval race with Germany and launched the dreadnought class of warship in 1906, provoking Germany to expand their navy in the **Third Naval Law**. Britain was determined to maintain naval supremacy.

- France also contributed to the arms race by expanding her army.

- Russia's decision to mobilise her army in July 1914 pushed Germany to enact the Schlieffen Plan.

- Without consulting Germany, Austria–Hungary created an international crisis in 1908 by annexing Bosnia. Austria antagonised Russia and Serbia during the crisis by threatening them with war. In 1914, Austria–Hungary was ultimately responsible for the decision to go to war with Serbia following the murder of Archduke Franz Ferdinand.

- The event that triggered the crisis that eventually caused the First World War did not originate in Germany: members of the Serbian Black Hand organisation organised the assassination.

- The **Balkan Wars** destabilised peace in Europe and these conflicts did not involve Germany. In 1912 and 1913, countries including Serbia, Montenegro, Greece, Bulgaria and Romania fought against the Ottoman Empire and among themselves for territorial control of the Balkan region. The Balkan Wars saw the Ottomans largely forced out of Europe and Serbia double in size.

The European system

Alliances

By 1914, the Great Powers of Europe were organised into two mutually antagonistic blocs.

Alliances were formed with a view to improving security and increasing co-operation, but they heightened tensions and ended up creating two opposed, hostile groups in Europe.

- In 1882, Germany, Austria–Hungary and Italy formed the **Triple Alliance** and agreed to support each other in the event of an attack by France or an attack by two or more other powers.

- In 1894, Russian concerns about the lapse of the Reinsurance Treaty and the Triple Alliance and France's desire to increase her security against German attack led France and Russia to create the **Franco-Russian Alliance**.

- In 1904 France and Britain later negotiated a co-operation agreement called the **Anglo-French Agreement** or *Entente Cordiale*.

- In 1907, Britain and Russia resolved some long-standing colonial agreements in the **Anglo-Russian Entente**.

- The agreements between Britain, France and Russia constituted the **Triple Entente**, a kind of loose alliance. None of the agreements were specifically aimed at challenging Germany, but the Triple Entente was interpreted by Germany as a threat. Many German military thinkers worried about encirclement.

The arms race and imperialism

In addition to the tensions caused by Britain and Germany's naval expansion, Germany, France and Russia were all involved in a build-up of their armies in the years before the First World War. The Army Bills of 1912 and 1913 increased the size of the German army by 20 per cent. In response, France decided to increase conscription from two to three years from 1916. Russia also had plans to increase their army by 500,000 from 1916.

Furthermore, Britain, France and Germany had all also been engaged in imperialist projects to build their empires. This imperial competition caused tension between the Great Powers of Europe.

Challenge the historian

Below is a source providing an interpretation of the causes of the First World War. You must read the source, identify the interpretation offered by the source, and use your own knowledge to provide a counter-argument, challenging the interpretation offered by the source.

SOURCE 1

(From Imanuel Geiss in Origins of the First World War, *published 1972)*

The ultimate responsibility falls on the ruling class in Austria–Hungary, less because it sent Franz Ferdinand into an 'alley of bomb-throwers' than on account of its inability to satisfy the legitimate struggle of their various nationalities for freedom, equality and social justice (a motive which is generally overlooked in the wholesale condemnation by Germany and Austria of the conspirators of Sarajevo). By their rigid adherence to outdated political and social conceptions, the traditional Powers left no room for the political agitations of the young south Slav intelligentsia who, in their desperation, were finally driven to the crime of political murder.

Interpretation offered by the source:

_____

_____

Counter-argument:

_____

_____

Write the question

The source above and the following sources relate to the extent to which Germany can be held responsible for the outbreak of the First World War. Read the guidance detailing what you need to know about this controversy. Having done this, write a Part (b) exam-style question using the sources.

SOURCE 2

(From William Mulligan in The Origins of the First World War, *published 2010)*

[Some] features of international politics reinforced the possibility of war. From 1911, the arms race in Europe escalated, as Germany, France, and Russia responded to each other's military challenge by increasing military expenditure and manpower. Other states, including the Balkan ones, also joined the race, so that states in Europe were locked in a web of escalating armaments. Diplomacy was militarised and the concept of the window of opportunity gained ground, as governments feared they would be unable to keep pace in the arms race with their rivals.

SOURCE 3

(From Niall Ferguson in The War of the World, *published 2006)*

The consensus has for many years been that it was the German government that wilfully turned the Balkan crisis of 1914 into a world war. Yet that is surely to understate the shared responsibility of all the European empires. For one thing, the Austrian government could hardly be blamed for demanding redress from Serbia in the wake of the Archduke's murder. Their alternate to Belgrade, delivered after much prevarication on July 23, essentially demanded that the Serbian authorities allow Austrian officials to participate in the inquiry into the assassinations. This was, all things considered, not an unreasonable demand. From a modern standpoint, the only European power to side with the victims of terrorism against the sponsors of terrorism was Germany.

Use Sources 1, 2 and 3 and your own knowledge.

How far do you agree that _____

_____

Explain your answer, using Sources 1, 2 and 3 and your own knowledge of the issues related to this controversy.

Possible interpretations

There are a number of possible interpretations of the causes of the First World War that could be advanced, which attribute varying degrees of responsibility to Germany.

Interpretation: the war was caused by a German desire for European hegemony

Germany pursued a war in order to become the dominant power in Europe. The War Council, September Programme and Schlieffen Plan indicate this. In the years before the First World War, Germany deliberately destabilised European peace and sought confrontation with the Entente powers, through, for example, the naval race with Britain and the antagonism against France during the Moroccan crises. When a crisis developed in the summer of 1914, the German military and political elite sought to capitalise on this, through encouraging Austrian aggression, hoping to escalate the conflict into a larger war.

Interpretation: 'escape forwards'

Some **structuralist** historians such as Wehler agreed with Fischer that Germany planned for an aggressive war. They added to Fischer's interpretation by arguing that German politicians sought a war in order to resolve domestic difficulties: to 'escape' from these problems by pushing forwards with an aggressive war. The government faced the problem of the stalemate caused by the growing power of the **SPD**, tensions caused by the Zabern Affair and a budget deficit. The conservative political and military elite sought to pursue war to strengthen their own position to try and create national unity, and to distract attention away from the need to reform the political system.

Interpretation: the war was caused by German fear of encirclement

The First World War was caused by German actions, such as their enactment of the Schlieffen Plan, but German actions were more **defensive** than aggressive. The Germans were responding to fears that the alliances between France, Russia and Britain and Russian and French plans to expand their army might mean that Germany could be crushed in the future by the Entente: Germany felt it faced an aggressive coalition. Many people in Germany accepted this as an explanation for the war. The Schlieffen Plan was Germany's only hope of victory if there was a possibility of France engaging on the side of Russia in a conflict between Russia and Germany.

Interpretation: 'calculated risk'

Another argument is that Germany did not so much have a long-term plan for an aggressive war as take a risk on war when the crisis developed in 1914. The German military and political elite took the chance to escalate the conflict between Austria and Serbia, as they hoped that they would gain easy victories. If a larger conflict developed, the Germans calculated that it was better to have a war sooner rather than later with the Entente powers, whose military expansion was not yet fully realised.

Interpretation: the war was caused by tensions, rivalry and instability between European countries

Many European powers contributed to destabilising peace in Europe in the years prior to the First World War. Alliances and agreements created tensions and suspicions and a number of countries contributed to the arms race. In the Balkans, the fallout from the weakening of Ottoman power caused conflict and ultimately triggered the war. In this context, European countries did not deliberately seek war, but in David Lloyd George's phrase 'slithered' almost accidently towards war.

Below are a sample Part (b) exam-style question and the sources referred to in the question. Read the question, study the sources and, using three coloured pens, underline them in Red, Amber and Green to show:

Red: Counter-arguments and counter-evidence provided by the source
Amber: Evidence that supports this interpretation
Green: The interpretation offered by the question

Use Sources 1, 2 and 3 and your own knowledge.

How far do you agree that the outbreak of the First World War was primarily due to the attitude of German generals who 'eagerly seized the opportunity for war' in 1914?

SOURCE 1

(From Hans-Ulrik Welher in The German Empire 1871–1918, *published 1997)*

Ruling elites who find themselves in a defensive position with their backs to the wall become greatly predisposed to taking considerable risks in order to hold on to their position of dominance. The key to the policy pursued by Germany's statesmen in the summer of 1914 lies in the predisposition of its ruling elites to continue their defensive struggle by aggressive means.

This predisposition, which had been growing increasingly since the second Moroccan crisis, was given the support of the influential high-ranking military at the decisive moment in time. Their arguments were the weight that tipped the balance in their decision to use the fresh Balkan crisis of 1914 as the lever for a spectacular foreign policy success which was intended to have a positive effect on Germany's internal situation. They therefore embarked upon a policy of 'escaping forwards' from the country's internal problems; they refused to place their trust in the gradually emerging, albeit long-drawn-out, procedures by which the Great Powers attempted to 'manage' such crises.

SOURCE 2

(From David G Herrmann in The Arming of Europe and the Making of the First World War, *published 1996)*

Between 1904 and 1914 a major change came about in the way European statesmen perceived military power, and that change made war a more likely outcome of the 1914 crisis than those in the preceding decade. The military environment in Europe went from a state of gradual peacetime development, relatively little heeded by civilian leaders, to one of intense competitive army increases explicitly directed at rival powers and constituting a major object of political concern. This transformation arose not only because of the land armaments race between 1912 and 1914, but also because of perceptions throughout the decade that the balance of military power among the states was changing. The policies that flowed from these perceptions, interacting with diplomatic alignments and crises, brought about the transformation by the time of the Sarajevo assassination in 1914.

SOURCE 3

(From Niall Ferguson in The War of the World, *published 2006)*

Without doubt, the German generals eagerly seized the opportunity for war and delayed their own mobilization only in order that Russia would appear the aggressor. Yet German anxieties about the pace of Russia's post-1905 rearmament were not wholly unjustified; there were legitimate reasons to fear that their Eastern neighbour was on the way to becoming militarily invincible. That was why Helmuth von Moltke, the Chief of the German General Staff, argued, insistently, that 'We would never again find a situation as favourable as now, when neither France nor Russia had completed the extension of their army organisation'.

 Recommended reading

Below is a list of suggested further reading on this topic.

- *1914: Why the World Went to War*, Niall Ferguson (2005)
- *The Origins of the First World War*, James Joll and Gordon Martel (2007)
- *The Origins of the First World War*, William Mulligan (2010)

Exam focus

On pages 35–37 is a sample answer to the Part (b) exam-style question on this page. Read the answer and the examiner comments around it.

(b) Use Sources 1, 2 and 3 and your own knowledge.

To what extent do you agree with the view that Germany's *Weltpolitik* was responsible for the outbreak of a general European war in August 1914?

Explain your answer, using Sources 1, 2 and 3 and your own knowledge of the issues related to this controversy. (40 marks)

SOURCE 1

(From Huw Strachan in The First World War: Volume I: To Arms, *published 2003)*

By 1914, the alliances had become a major vehicle for the expression of a great power's status. This was the context into which Germany's *Weltpolitik* fitted. By 1914 Germany simultaneously sought affirmation as a world power and as a continental power. Furthermore, it did so in a way calculated to infuriate. Bethmann Hollweg put a large share of the blame for the war on his own country: 'the earlier errors of a Turkish policy against Russia, a Moroccan against France, naval policy against England, irritating everyone, blockading everybody's way and yet not really weakening anyone.' By July 1914 each power, conscious in a self-absorbed way of its own potential weakness, felt it was on its mettle, that its status as a great power would be forfeit if it failed to act.

SOURCE 2

(From David G Herrmann in The Arming of Europe and the Making of the First World War, *published 1996)*

In none of the diplomatic crises between 1905 and 1914 did statesmen enter confrontations with the intent to provoke a war, or even to threaten their advisories with one. Once the crises came to a head, however, the principal decision makers often did menace their opponents with war and almost invariably took the balance of military power into consideration. This did not mean that the strategic situation dictated the outcome of all crises. In 1914, however, perceptions of military strength did have a strong influence on the decisions for war. This was partly because statesmen perceived that windows of opportunity were closing, and partly because the armaments competition of the preceding two years had forced even civilian leaders to think extensively about military power long before the crisis itself made war an immediate prospect.

SOURCE 3

(From James Joll and Gordon Martell in The Origins of the First World War, *published 2007)*

The relations between internal and external policies in the main belligerent countries suggests that no single explanatory model is applicable to all of them, and that in almost every case the decision for war was the result of contradictory hopes, fears, inherited attitudes and previous plans rather than of cool and rational calculation of profit and loss. In the short term, considerations of domestic policy obviously played their part and differed much between one country and another. In Germany the government was under pressure from the Right, in Britain and France from the Left, so that such estimates as were made about the effects of war on the internal situation were bound to be different. Still, it is true that the war did in fact appear in its first stages to supply a solution to many problems.

Undoubtedly, as Source 1 argues, by 1914 Germany's Weltpolitik was the context in which rivalry between the major powers was played out, and therefore an important cause of the outbreak of war in Europe in August 1914. Source 3, although reluctant to attribute the cause of the First World War to any individual factor, points to the relationship between domestic and international concerns in the minds of European statesmen as a cause of the war. Source 2, by contrast, argues that all European powers share the blame because their 'perceptions of military strength' led them to take a calculated risk and embrace a general European war when the opportunity arose in the middle of 1914. Ultimately, 'perceptions of military strength' (Source 2) in Germany were the decisive factor as the belief that Germany could win the war, achieve its Weltpolitik aims, and appease domestic opinion, led to the outbreak of the First World War.

Source 1 argues that German Weltpolitik had become the context in which the Great European Powers competed for dominance, and was therefore the prime cause of the First World War. Weltpolitik (world politics) was the policy of seeking a more dominant position in Europe and colonial expansion. It entailed a rise in German nationalism at home, and a more aggressive policy towards its European neighbours. Source 1 argues that Weltpolitik made other European powers conscious of their 'own potential weakness' and therefore more willing to go to war to defend their Great Power status against Germany's increasing strength. Source 3 backs this up, by arguing that 'the decision for war was the result of contradictory hopes, fears, inherited attitudes and previous plans' alluding to the concerns of Britain, France and Russia in the face of an increasingly self-confident Germany. These tensions were particularly clear in the Moroccan Crises of 1905–1911, during which Germany attempted to wrest control of Morocco from the French Empire. Indeed, at the end of the Moroccan Crises Germany won the right to control parts of the Congo, which represented a significant increase in Germany's colonial power. Source 1's reference to the importance of Weltpolitik ignores an important aspect of the policy picked up by Source 3. Source 3 refers to the domestic impact of Weltpolitik noting that 'the government was under pressure from the right' to deliver on its Weltpolitik goals. In this sense too, Weltpolitik pushed Germany to adopt an aggressive stance in its dealings with other European powers to maintain domestic support for the Kaiser's government. Nonetheless, while Weltpolitik was important in setting the context for war, it was not the trigger for war as Weltpolitik had been a consistent policy since 1896.

The introduction refers to the interpretations offered by all three of the sources and provides an immediate answer to the question. This shows focus on the sources, alongside independence of thought.

Each of the main paragraphs begins with reference to the interpretations offered by the sources. In this sense, the sources are used to shape the argument of the essay.

Here, the candidate links the sources to their own knowledge, constructing an integrated response to the question.

At the end of each paragraph, the candidate links back to the question, showing sustained focus.

This paragraph begins by discussing another possible interpretation of the causes of the First World War. It is important that Part (b) essays consider a range of possible interpretations.

Source 2 argues that 'perceptions of military strength' had an important impact on the decisions of the major powers to go to war. Essentially, Source 2 argues that European powers saw a 'window of opportunity' during the summer of 1914, when each calculated that they had the best chance of winning a European war. This was particularly true of Germany, which had been pursuing Weltpolitik since the turn of the century. Source 1 acknowledges that German Weltpolitik had enraged Germany's neighbours, quoting Bethmann Hollweg who acknowledges the 'errors of a Turkish policy against Russia, a Moroccan policy against France, a naval policy against England.' Therefore, German statesmen believed that war was inevitable and were prepared to take a calculated risk in August 1914, believing it to be their best chance of winning this war. Indeed, Germany's decision to implement the Schlieffen Plan in August 1914 was an attempt to seize the advantage, before Russia had mobilised, and force the Triple Entente to accept peace on Germany's terms, recognising their dominance in Europe and allowing them to expand in Africa. Therefore, Source 2 is wrong to argue that all European powers were looking for a 'window of opportunity.'

Here, the candidate challenges the interpretation offered by Source 2, showing independence of thought. The challenge is not just asserted, but explained.

As Source 1 argues, European powers were increasingly responding to Germany's Weltpolitik, rather than pursuing their own European goals. It was Germany, consistent with its Weltpolitik, and conscious of its temporary military advantage, that was prepared to take a calculated risk. Therefore, 'perceptions of military strength' (Source 2) were the trigger for war, but primarily among German policy makers, who seized the opportunity and mobilised in order to secure Germany's 'place in the sun.'

Here, the sources are used in combination, to form a fully integrated response.

Source 3 usefully links international and domestic policy, noting that all European governments were under pressure from their own people to go to war. This is supported, to some extent, by Source 2, which argues that the arms race between the major European powers between 1912 and 1914 'had forced even civilian leaders' to consider war in the run-up to the July Crisis. Domestic pressure was most significant in Germany. The Hottentot election of 1906, the Daily Telegraph Affair of 1908, and the Zabern Affair of 1912 all indicated that the Kaiser, and his Weltpolitik, were under pressure from the left, as well as the right, as noted in Source 3. This points to another cause for war.

The candidate's own knowledge used is detailed, showing a confident grasp of the topic.

Structuralist historians have argued that the German government embraced war in order to 'escape forward', that is to say, to resolve domestic difficulties by uniting the German people in a war designed to ensure German greatness. Notably, it was Bethmann Hollweg who urged the Austrians to take swift military action against the Serbians. Bethmann Hollweg was under pressure in the Reichstag, particularly from the political left, and therefore had reasons rooted in domestic politics for putting pressure on the Austrians to go to war. However, Weltpolitik also played a role in negotiations with the Austrians as Generals Ludendorff and Hindenburg hoped that a conflict between Austria and Serbia would lead to war between Germany and Russia, which would allow Germany to gain territory in the East. Clearly, there were domestic issues involved in Germany's decision to go to war. However, the July Crisis was the first crisis emerging from Weltpolitik in which Germany's military leaders were convinced they could win a general war in Europe and therefore 'perceptions of military strength' (Source 2) were more significant than domestic pressures.

In conclusion, as Source 1 argues, Weltpolitik was certainly an important factor in the outbreak of a general European war in 1914. In essence, Weltpolitik set the context for relations between Great European Powers, forcing Britain and France on to their 'mettle' and making a European conflict more likely. Source 3 is also correct that domestic politics played a role, as the German government saw war as a way of appeasing the right and pacifying the left. However the crucial factor was the perception of relative military strength discussed in Source 2. While this was not as pervasive outside Germany as Source 2 would suggest, it was extremely important at the top of German government. The belief that Germany could win a general European war, and in so doing gain its 'place in the sun' and consolidate its domestic support, meant that German policy makers seized the opportunity presented by the July crisis and launched a war in Europe.

The conclusion explains the relative importance of the different factors discussed, and makes links to all of the sources. Therefore, the essay concludes with a reasoned judgement.

38/40

This essay presents a sustained analytical response from own knowledge, showing an explicit understanding of the issues raised by the question. It integrates own knowledge with material from the sources. The sources are used with confidence, presenting and criticising the interpretations that they offer, in order to develop an independent argument. The answer does not get full marks as the own knowledge is not extensive for an answer of this level.

Reverse engineering

The best essays are based on careful plans. Read the essay and the examiner's comments and try to work out the general points of the plan used to write the essay. Once you have done this, note down the specific examples used to support each general point.

Section 3: The democratic experiment, 1919–1929

The Weimar constitution

Revised

A new system

Following elections in January 1919, a National Assembly met in the city of Weimar to form an interim parliament and to agree a new constitution. The largest party in the Assembly was the **SPD**, which had won 38 per cent of the vote. SPD representatives wished to create a democracy which secured rights for workers, but they had to co-operate with the other pro-democracy parties, such as the Centre Party and the DDP (German Democratic Party). They agreed a liberal democratic system with protections for workers.

The Weimar Republic

This is the name often given to Germany between 1919 and 1933. It refers to a period of democracy in Germany and takes its name from the city where the new constitution was agreed. The Weimar Republic had two presidents, Friedrich Ebert (1919–1925) and Paul von Hindenburg (1925–1934).

The constitution

Some of the main features of Weimar's constitutional arrangements were as follows:

- A President was to be elected every seven years, with the power to select and dismiss the Chancellor. The Chancellor formed the government.
- The President was Supreme Commander of the Armed Forces.
- The President could **dissolve** the lower house of the German parliament, the Reichstag, and call new Reichstag elections under Article 25 of the constitution. The new elections had to occur within 60 days of the dissolution.
- The Chancellor and government were accountable to the Reichstag and had to resign if they lost the confidence of the Reichstag.

- The Reichstag was to be elected every four years. There was **universal suffrage** for people over the age of 20.
- Elections were to be conducted using **proportional representation**: the minimum requirement for a seat in the Reichstag was just 60,000 votes across the entire country.
- A **federal** system: Germany was divided into eighteen regions or states, each of which had its own parliament and local powers. The state parliaments sent representatives to the Reichsrat, the upper house of the German parliament. The Reichsrat could propose amendments, or delay **legislation** passed by the Reichstag.
- **Referenda** on single issues could be held if enough people petitioned for one.

The Bill of Rights

The Weimar Republic's constitution also included a **Bill of Rights** in which certain rights were **enshrined**. These provisions included:

- freedoms of speech, association and religion
- the right to work (the government should ensure that everyone had a job or, failing that, provide financial assistance)
- a provision giving workers special protection in the new state
- welfare rights (such as protection for the disabled)
- the right to own property (meaning businesses could not be **nationalised** without compensation).

Emergency provisions

Under Article 48 of the constitution, the President had the power to rule via presidential **decree** in the event of an emergency. However, this power was checked as the Reichstag could review and overturn any decree issued under Article 48.

Mind map

Use the information on the opposite page to add detail to the mind map below.

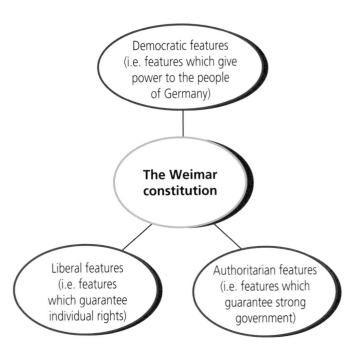

Democratic features (i.e. features which give power to the people of Germany)

The Weimar constitution

Liberal features (i.e. features which guarantee individual rights)

Authoritarian features (i.e. features which guarantee strong government)

Complete the paragraph

Below are a sample Part (a) exam-style question and a paragraph written in answer to this question. The paragraph contains a point and specific examples, but lacks a concluding explanatory link back to the question. Complete the paragraph, adding this link in the space provided.

'The Weimar constitution was too democratic to ensure stable government.'
How far do you agree with this opinion?

One feature of the Weimar constitution which was designed to guarantee stable government was Article 48. This article could be invoked by the President at times of emergency. Essentially, Article 48 gave the President the power to rule by decree in an emergency. This power was subject to the Reichstag. In practice, this meant that the Reichstag needed to authorise the use of Article 48, and that the Reichstag could review the use of Article 48 by overturning any emergency decrees that the President issued.

_____

_____

The nature of the Weimar Republic's constitution

The nature of the Weimar Republic's constitution has been controversial. Did the system collapse after only fourteen years because the constitution was flawed, or was the constitution a good one which was misused by politicians? It was a remarkably democratic system, but one which also tended to produce weak government.

Democratic features

One notable feature of Weimar Germany's constitution was its very democratic character:

- The President, the head of state, was elected.
- There was universal suffrage, as women and young men were enfranchised for the first time, and the government was now accountable to the elected Reichstag, unlike in the Second Reich.
- Proportional representation produced very democratic results as the number of seats allocated in the Reichstag reflected almost exactly the preferences of voters.
- Also, an element of **direct democracy** was included in the constitutional provision which allowed for referenda.
- The President appointed the Chancellor, but as the government needed to have Reichstag support, it became the norm for members of the Reichstag to be selected as Chancellor. This gave the government a more democratic character and represented a change from the Second Reich where unelected *Junkers* had generally been appointed.
- The constitution also contained **checks and balances** which enhanced its democratic credentials; no one part of the political system should have been able to become too powerful: the electorate held the Reichstag to account, the President could dismiss the Reichstag but needed the Reichstag's support to get the government's agenda into law.
- The Bill of Rights also contained liberal features that helped to support democracy such as freedom of speech (which ensured a free press) and freedom of association (which meant that people were free to participate in politics via political parties, trade unions or **pressure groups**).

Criticisms of the Weimar Republic's constitution

The Weimar constitution has been criticised for giving too much power to the President under Articles 25 and 48, although both of these provisions contained limitations on the President's power. Proportional representation has been condemned for creating a fragmented party system which made it difficult to form durable coalition governments and within which small extremist parties could gain representation and exposure: there were twenty separate coalition governments in Weimar Germany.

Supporters and opponents of the Weimar Republic's constitution

Supporters	• The pro-Weimar parties were the SPD, Centre Party and DDP: these parties won a majority in the 1919 elections. • After 1920, the DVP (German People's Party) started to support Weimar.
Opponents	• The conservative DVP initially opposed Weimar as they wished for a constitutional monarchy. • The right-wing DNVP (German Nationalist People's Party) wavered in their support for Weimar and were mainly opposed prior to 1925 and after 1929. • Many industrialists and business owners in Germany felt that the constitution gave too many rights to workers and by the early 1930s many of these people had stopped supporting the Weimar system, as they felt it did not serve their interests.

Simple essay style

Below is a sample Part (a) exam-style question. Use your own knowledge and the information on the opposite page to produce a plan for this question. Choose four general points, and provide three pieces of specific information to support each general point. Once you have planned your essay, write the introduction and conclusion for the essay. The introduction should list the points to be discussed in the essay. The conclusion should summarise the key points and justify which point was the most important.

How democratic was the Weimar constitution?

Develop the detail

Below is a sample Part (a) exam-style question and a paragraph written in answer to this question. The paragraph contains a limited amount of detail. Annotate the paragraph to add additional detail to the answer.

'Weimar democracy never enjoyed the support of the majority of the German people.' How far do you agree with this opinion?

There was much dissatisfaction with the Weimar constitution from the right wing of German politics. For example, the Junkers were excluded from some branches of government. Equally, conservative political parties opposed the Weimar constitution. Additionally, industrialists and business owners objected to the Weimar constitution. Also, the democratic nature of the constitution concerned businessmen. In this way, the Weimar constitution did not enjoy the majority of support from the right wing because there were concerns that it was too democratic and gave too much power to the workers.

The problems of Weimar Germany 1919–1922: the legacy of the Second Reich and the First World War

Weimar Germany had been born of revolution, defeat and social and economic turmoil. Consequently, in its first years, the Republic struggled to overcome various political and economic challenges.

The legacy of the First World War

Defeat in the First World War created a number of problems for the new democracy. Democratic politicians had no real option but to sign the **armistice** which ended the First World War in November 1918. Many Germans then unfairly blamed the democratic politicians for the defeat and labelled them the '**November Criminals**'. The '**stab in the back myth**', which falsely portrayed the cause of the German loss to have been the revolution and betrayal by democratic and socialist politicians, was widely believed in some sections of German society, and served to undermine support for Weimar Germany. When the **Treaty of Versailles** was signed, disillusionment with the new Republic set in as, despite the formation of the new democracy, a **punitive** peace treaty had been imposed. An additional negative legacy of the war was that its cost produced **inflation**, which contributed to post-war economic problems.

The Treaty of Versailles

The Treaty of Versailles was the peace treaty between Germany and her opponents in the First World War. As part of the Treaty:

- Germany's army was restricted to 100,000 men.
- Only six battleships, and no submarines or air force, were permitted.
- Germany lost territory, including its overseas colonies and West Posen and West **Prussia** to newly created Poland, and Alsace and Lorraine to France.
- The Rhineland, which bordered France, was **demilitarised** and the Saarland placed under **League of Nations** control.
- Union with Austria, **_Anschluss_**, was banned and Germany had to accept liability for the war in the 'War Guilt' clause and pay **reparations** to the victors for damages incurred during the war. In 1921, it was decided that the total amount of reparations would be 269 billion gold **marks**.

The Treaty was widely reviled in Germany as a 'diktat', or dictated peace.

Lack of public support for democracy

Another problem faced by Weimar was that the new democratic system did not have the wholehearted support of the majority of Germans. The first election in 1919 produced a majority for the pro-Weimar parties but the 1920 election saw their support slump to only 45 per cent.

The persistence of the old regime

A further issue was that many of the Second Reich's old elite remained in place. In 1918, the radical socialist **USPD** had called for the comprehensive removal of these people from positions of power. However, moderates in the SPD, seeking to promote stability and avoid the possibility of army rebellion, chose instead to reach a compromise. This deal left the armed forces, judiciary and civil service unreformed, still dominated by the old elite. These elements from the old regime at times undermined democracy. In 1920, the army did not support the government during the **Kapp Putsch** (see page 44), and the judiciary's response to the right-wing rebellions was weak: Hitler, found guilty of **treason** in 1924 after the **Munich Putsch** (see page 58),was only sentenced to five years in jail and served only nine months. The lack of support for the new system from some in the elite undermined it.

Introducing an argument

Below are a sample Part (a) exam-style question, a list of key points to be made in the essay, and a simple introduction and conclusion for the essay. Read the question, the plan, and the introduction and conclusion. Rewrite the introduction and the conclusion in order to develop an argument.

To what extent was Germany a liberal democracy in the years 1919–1929?

Key points:

- Liberal features of the constitution
- Democratic features of the constitution
- Authoritarian features of the constitution

Introduction

Between 1919 and 1929 Germany had liberal features and democratic features. In addition, it had authoritarian features.

Conclusion

Between 1919 and 1929 Germany had liberal features and democratic features. In addition, it had authoritarian features. Overall, it was a liberal democracy to a fair extent.

Eliminate irrelevance

Below are a sample Part (a) exam-style question and a paragraph written in answer to this question. Read the paragraph and identify parts of the paragraph that are not directly relevant to the question. Draw a line through the information that is irrelevant and justify your deletions in the margin.

'The prime factor that undermined the stability of Weimar Germany in the period 1919 to 1924 was the association of the Weimar regime with defeat in the First World War.' How far do you agree with this view?

One way in which defeat in the First World War did undermine the stability of Weimar Germany in the period 1919 to 1924 was the association between the new government and the 'November Criminals'. The war had been caused by many factors, including the rivalry between Great Powers and the arms race. German generals protected themselves from public criticism by alleging that they were betrayed by politicians who forced them to accept the terms of the armistice and later betrayed Germany by accepting reparations and full responsibility for the outbreak of the First World War. German generals had taken over the running of the government in 1916, forming the 'Silent Dictatorship' which sidelined Wilhelm II from his own government. Consequently, democratic politicians who had established the Weimar constitution were labelled the 'November Criminals' by their opponents in order to discredit the new democracy. However, it was wrong to criticise German politicians because, as Fritz Fischer has argued, Germany was indeed responsible for the First World War. In this way, the association between the Weimar Republic and defeat in the First World War undermined the stability of German democracy because, from the very beginning, democratic politicians were considered criminals who had betrayed their own country.

The problems of Weimar 1919–1922: political extremists

Political extremists from right and left rejected democracy and constituted a significant threat to the Weimar Republic.

The threat from the extreme left

Some on the extreme left wished to see Germany become a communist state like the **Soviet Union**. Therefore, they sought to destroy the Weimar Republic.

The Spartacist uprising 1919

In 1919 the communist political group, the Spartacists, took advantage of a large political protest in Berlin to launch an attempted communist revolution. President Ebert ordered the paramilitary **Freikorps**, volunteer groups of armed ex-servicemen, to crush the attempted rebellion. The leaders of the Spartacists, Rosa Luxemburg and Karl Liebknecht, were killed.

Strikes, risings and communist takeover

Widespread strike action and communist street violence contributed to the political instability of the early 1920s. Communists also temporarily took control or rebelled in a number of areas of Germany: Bavaria in 1919, the Ruhr in 1920 and Saxony and Thuringia in 1923. As a result of the **Ebert–Groener Pact**, the army and sometimes the Freikorps acted to crush these rebellions.

Fear of communism

The activities of **left-wing** revolutionaries and the success of the communist takeover in Russia caused many to fear communist revolution in Germany. This fear of communism led some to overlook the threat posed by the extreme right who in reality were the larger danger.

The threat from the extreme right

Those on the extreme right wanted a more authoritarian system and tried to undermine or destroy the new democracy.

The Kapp Putsch, 1920

Following the disbandment of a Freikorps group as part of post-war disarmament, a group of right-wing politicians and soldiers, led by Wolfgang Kapp, seized control of Berlin. The government fled to Stuttgart. The Putsch had little support from the public or the elite and quickly collapsed following a general strike.

Another example of a right-wing attempt to overthrow Weimar was the Munich Putsch, 1923 (covered on page 58).

White terror: assassinations and violence

Anti-Weimar paramilitary groups carried out a wave of political assassinations between 1919 and 1922 and created a destabilising atmosphere of violence on the streets of Germany as they launched violent attacks on political opponents. A total of 354 political assassinations were carried out by right-wing death squads, primarily the group Organisation Consul, including the murder of prominent politicians, such as former finance minister and Centre Party member Matthias Erzberger in 1921 and foreign minister and industrialist Walther Rathenau in 1922.

Political assassinations

The judiciary's response to the white terror indicates that judges tended to favour right-wing extremists:

- Between January 1919 and 24 June 1922, 354 murders were committed by sympathisers of the right.
- Of these murders, 326 went unpunished. Only one life sentence and a total of 90 years in prisons were handed out.
- By comparison, 22 murders were committed by sympathisers of the left.
- Of these murders, four went unpunished, and ten death sentences, three life sentences and a total of 250 years in prison were handed out.

The 'stab in the back' myth

The nationalist right did not just undermine Weimar through direct action: the 'stab in the back' myth had a pernicious influence in that it made democracy appear weak and un-German and portrayed democratic politicians as traitors.

Spot the mistake

Below are a sample Part (a) exam-style question and a paragraph written in answer to this question. Why does this paragraph not get into Level 4? Once you have identified the mistake, rewrite the paragraph so that it displays the qualities of Level 4. The mark scheme on page 117 will help you.

'The biggest threat to Weimar democracy in the years 1919 to 1924 was the extreme left.' How far do you agree with this opinion?

> The extreme left did pose a threat to Weimar democracy. In 1919, Germany witnessed the Spartacist uprising. The Spartacists were led by Rosa Luxemburg and Karl Liebknecht. They wanted a communist government in Germany similar to the communist government in Russia. They took over large areas of Berlin, establishing communist control. President Ebert would not tolerate the threat from the extreme left and sent in the Freikorps to crush the rebellion. In the end, the Spartacists were unsuccessful and its leaders were killed. In addition, between 1919 and 1923, there were strikes and communist violence in Bavaria, the Ruhr, in Saxony, and in Thuringia. Again, Ebert turned to the Freikorps for help and the rebellions were quashed.

 Introducing an argument

Below are a sample Part (a) exam-style question, a list of key points to be made in the essay, and a simple introduction and conclusion for the essay. Read the question, the plan, and the introduction and conclusion. Rewrite the introduction and the conclusion in order to develop an argument.

'The biggest threat to Weimar democracy in the years 1919 to 1924 was the extreme left.' How far do you agree with this opinion?

Key points

- Revolt from the extreme left
- Opposition from the extreme right
- The 'stab in the back' myth
- The nature of the Weimar constitution

Introduction

> There were a number of key threats to Weimar democracy in the years 1919 to 1924. These were revolts from the left, opposition from the extreme right, the 'stab in the back' myth, and the nature of the Weimar constitution.

Conclusion

> There were a number of key threats to Weimar democracy in the years 1919 to 1924. The most important threat was the revolts from the extreme left. This was a more significant threat than all of the other factors.

1923 – year of crisis

Revised

In 1923, many of the political and economic problems of Weimar Germany reached crisis point, as inflation spiralled out of control, the Ruhr was invaded and the Nazis attempted to overthrow the government.

The inflationary problem

Wartime and demobilisation inflation

- The First World War left Germany with high inflation: much of the cost of the war had been financed by increasing the money supply and the German currency consequently declined in value.
- Wartime shortages exacerbated the problem and caused price rises.
- In the aftermath of the war, government expenditure remained high as the government had to support war widows, injured war veterans and **demobilised** soldiers.
- Furthermore, the new constitution made social security a constitutional right, which obligated the government to provide support to the unemployed.

Reparations

From 1921, the problem increased with the start of reparations payments:

- One difficulty Germany faced in meeting its reparations obligations was that most of the reparations had to be paid for in gold marks, which held their value as the currency declined.
- As inflation increased and the value of the German currency weakened, paying for reparations became an ever more expensive burden.
- In 1922, the German government sought to suspend their reparations payments, but were refused permission.
- By early 1923, Germany was failing to meet all of its reparations obligations.

The Ruhr crisis

In January 1923 the French and Belgian governments responded to German failure to meet all reparations payments by ordering the invasion of the German industrial region, the Ruhr. Their armies occupied factories and mines and seized raw materials and goods in lieu of reparations. With government support, workers and business owners in the Ruhr followed a policy of **passive resistance**, refusing to co-operate with the occupying forces by going on strike. The German government paid the workers and compensated owners for lost revenue, thus adding to government expenditure. The situation in the Ruhr further damaged the German economy.

Hyperinflation

The already profound problem of inflation in Germany ran out of control in the aftermath of the Ruhr crisis as confidence in the German currency collapsed: the mark now became worthless. To try to meet spending obligations, the government printed more and more money, adding to the problem. In 1923, 300 paper mills and 150 printing presses worked 24 hours a day to print money. While the new government of Gustav Stresemann struggled to resolve the situation, the Nazis launched a failed putsch in Munich in November 1923 (see page 58). In the end the issue of hyperinflation was resolved (see page 48) but not without causing a great shock to Germans, many of whom saw their savings eradicated or standard of living dramatically reduced. Debtors, who included many large business owners, benefited however, as the value of their debts was wiped out by hyperinflation.

Inflation in Germany 1919–23 – marks needed to buy one US dollar

Apr 1919	Nov 1921	Aug 1922	Jan 1923	Sept 1923	Dec 1923
12	263	1000	17,000	98,860,000	4,200,000,000,000 (i.e. 4.2 trillion)

Eliminate irrelevance

Below are a sample Part (a) exam-style question and a paragraph written in answer to this question. Read the paragraph and identify parts of the paragraph that are not directly relevant to the question. Draw a line through the information that is irrelevant and justify your deletions in the margin.

'The main threats to the stability of the Weimar Republic in the period 1919 to 1923 were economic rather than political.' How far do you agree with this view?

Reparations were a major economic threat to the stability of the Weimar Republic in the period 1919 to 1924. The Treaty of Versailles stipulated that Germany had to pay reparations for the damage caused in the First World War. Germany had lost the war as a result of economic problems and poor leadership. In 1921, the total amount of reparations was set at 269 billion gold marks. In order to pay reparations and keep their economy afloat, the German government began to print money. By 1923, 300 paper mills and 150 printing presses worked day and night to create paper currency, leading to hyperinflation. This was the opposite of the economic problems that affected Germany at the end of the 1920s, when the Wall Street Crash led to a Depression. As a result, the mark became almost valueless. For example, in April 1919, 12 marks were needed to buy $1. However, by December 1923, 4.2 trillion marks were needed to buy $1. Consequently, the economic crisis led to the eradication of the savings of many Germans. Fortunately, the Dawes Plan of 1924 agreed staged repayments of the reparations bill, and massive American loans which diffused the situation, decreasing tensions within Germany. In this way, economic crisis led to political instability as the German public blamed their government for the decrease in their standard of living.

Develop the detail

Below are a sample Part (a) exam-style question and a paragraph written in answer to this question. The paragraph contains a limited amount of detail. Annotate the paragraph to add additional detail to the answer.

'The main threats to the stability of the Weimar Republic in the period 1919 to 1923 were economic rather than political.' How far do you agree with this view?

The Ruhr crisis shows the interrelation of political and economic problems which destabilised the Weimar Republic. The crisis was caused by the failure of Germany to meet its reparation payments. As a result, France and Belgium invaded the Ruhr, determined to seize reparations by force. The German government resisted the invasion. As a result, there was an economic crisis. The Ruhr crisis led to hyperinflation and the value of the mark dropped. Thus, the political crisis of a foreign invasion led to the economic crisis of hyperinflation, both of which destabilised the Weimar Republic by demonstrating the weakness of the new government.

How did the Weimar Republic survive its early problems?

Despite political violence, attempted revolution, financial crisis and invasion, Weimar survived its early period due to the weakness of the opposition and the actions of some of its politicians.

The weakness of Weimar's opponents

Weimar's opponents were disunited, often having different political goals. Additionally they lacked effective organisation and widespread support.

Poor leadership and planning of attempted putsches

■ The Spartacists did not carefully plan their attempted takeover of power, as Lenin had in Russia, but opportunistically tried to turn a protest into a revolution.

■ During the Munich Putsch, Hitler exhibited indecision as he dithered overnight about whether to launch his **coup**, which gave time to others to alert the authorities. In addition, the route marched during the Putsch, down a fairly narrow street, allowed the Bavarian police to trap the rebels and defeat them.

Lack of support from the public

Despite the ambivalence that many Germans felt for the Republic, there was not widespread support for extremists. The Spartacists had only around 15,000 members and a huge general strike brought down the government established by Kapp. Some 700,000 people demonstrated in Berlin against political violence following the murder of Walther Rathenau in 1922 and it was this public revulsion rather than police or judicial action that ended the assassinations.

The actions of Ebert and Stresemann

President Ebert

Ebert acted ruthlessly against the Spartacists and other left-wing rebels. He also led the call for a general strike in Berlin during the Kapp Putsch. Ebert ruled under Article 48 during the Munich Putsch, which enabled him to take control of the situation.

Gustav Stresemann

As Chancellor, Stresemann helped to solve the crisis of 1923 by calling off passive resistance to French occupation. This reduced government payments and calmed the situation. Stresemann recognised that international confidence in Germany would only be restored if Germany met its obligations and so he restarted reparations payments. To pay for this, government spending was cut (700,000 state employees were sacked) and Stresemann worked to negotiate the Dawes Plan, which alleviated the burden of reparations payments and provided US loans and investment to assist the German economy. In addition, Stresemann worked with banker Hjalmar Schacht and finance minister Hans Luther to resolve inflation. The old currency was abolished and a new currency, the **Rentenmark**, was established. One unit of the new currency was worth 1 trillion of the old. **Collateral** for the new currency was provided by linking the new currency to German industrial and agricultural assets.

The Dawes Plan, 1924

Banker Charles Dawes led an international committee which redesigned reparations. The annual payment of gold marks was reduced to 1 million, rising to 2.5 million from 1929. An international loan was made available to help Germany pay.

Other factors helping Weimar Germany's survival

■ **The elite**: Despite the ambivalence of many in the elite for the new political system, some members of the elite helped it to survive. The army enthusiastically crushed left-wing rebellions and supported the government during the Munich Putsch. The civil service and banking community refused to co-operate with the Kapp government.

■ **Support from the international community**: The Dawes Plan of 1924 helped to stabilise the German economy and currency.

Spectrum of significance

Below are a sample Part (a) exam-style question and a list of general points which could be used to answer the question. Use your own knowledge and the information in this section to reach a judgement about the importance of these general points to the question posed. Write numbers on the spectrum below to indicate their relative importance. Having done this, write a brief justification of your placement, explaining why some of these factors are more important than others. The resulting diagram could form the basis of an essay plan.

How far do you agree that the main reason for the survival of the Weimar government in the years 1919 to 1924 was the weaknesses of its opponents?

1. Weaknesses of opponents on the left wing
2. Weaknesses of opponents on the right wing
3. The Ebert–Groener Pact
4. Popular support for democracy

5. The Dawes Plan
6. The actions of Stresemann
7. The actions of President Ebert

Very important   Less important

 Developing an argument

Below are a sample Part (a) exam-style question, a list of key points to be made in the essay, and a paragraph from the essay. Read the question, the plan, and the sample paragraph. Rewrite the paragraph in order to develop an argument. Your paragraph should explain why the factor discussed in the paragraph is either the most significant factor or less significant than another factor.

How far do you agree that the main reason for the survival of the Weimar government in the years 1919 to 1924 was the weaknesses of its opponents?

Key points

- Weaknesses of opponents on the left wing
- Weaknesses of opponents on the right wing
- The Ebert–Groener Pact
- Popular support for democracy

- The Dawes Plan
- The actions of Stresemann
- The actions of President Ebert

Sample paragraph

One reason for the survival of the Weimar government in the years 1919 to 1924 was the actions of Stresemann. Appointed as Chancellor in 1923, Stresemann immediately called off the passive resistance in the Ruhr that had been initiated by Ebert. This meant that German industry in the Ruhr could begin production again, the German economy could start to make money, and French and Belgian forces could withdraw. Stresemann also stabilised the government by reducing government spending. For example, he sacked 700,000 government employees, which cut the government's wages bill. In order to solve the problem of hyperinflation, and thereby restabilise the government, Stresemann employed banker and economist Hjalmar Schacht, who abolished the old currency and introduced the Rentenmark, which was linked to the value of German industrial and farming assets and therefore remained stable in value. In this way, Stresemann's actions helped the Weimar government survive, because they solved the major economic problems of the early 1920s.

1924–1929: 'Golden Years'– politics and economics

1924–1929 saw economic improvements and greater political stability in Germany. During these 'Golden Years', support for democracy increased and Germany gained acceptance in the international community. Underneath the apparently stable and successful surface, however, Germany still had a great many problems.

Were the golden years really so golden?

	Positive features	Negative features
Politics	**Increased political stability** • No putsch attempts. • No political assassinations. • The creation of the **Grand Coalition** in 1928: this coalition, led by the SPD's Müller, was a coalition of the left, right and centre and commanded a secure majority (over 60 per cent) in the Reichstag. **Increased acceptance of democracy** • By the 1928 election, 76 per cent of people supported pro-Weimar parties. • Support for the Nazis was low: they obtained only 2.6 per cent of the vote in 1928. • A far right coalition failed to get support in their anti-Young Plan referendum. **The role of Hindenburg** • Despite his authoritarian past, President Hindenburg upheld the new constitution and, in 1928, chose a SPD Chancellor in spite of his hostility to **socialism**.	**Immature party politics and unstable coalitions** • Political parties did not co-operate well. The SPD were often reluctant to work with others, while governments were sometimes brought down by apparently trivial issues, such as the collapse of Luther's 1926 administration over the appearance of the German flag. • Forming stable coalition governments proved difficult: the centre right and right could agree on domestic policies but not foreign policies, while the centre right and left could agree on foreign policy but not domestic policies. There were consequently seven governments during 1923–1929 and some governments did not have majority support in the Reichstag. **Extremist support** • Support for extremists reduced but remained high with a quarter of people voting for parties that wished to see Weimar democracy end: the KPD, the German Communist Party, obtained 10.6 per cent of the vote in 1928. **The role of Hindenburg** • Hindenburg was hostile to the idea of working with the SPD before 1928 and until that time insisted that the far right DNVP be included in coalitions.
Economics	**Economic growth and development** • By 1928, production equalled that of 1913. • By 1928, national income was 12 per cent higher than in 1913. • Certain sectors of the economy performed particularly well: chemicals company IG Farben became the largest manufacturer in Europe. • Exports rose by 40 per cent between 1925 and 1929. • Loans from the international community, particularly the USA, financed the development of infrastructure in Germany: 25.5 billion marks were loaned between 1924 and 1930. • Inflation remained relatively low. • Unemployment ran at a relatively low level. **Improved standards of living** • Wages rose every year between 1924 and 1930.	**A sluggish agricultural sector** • Agriculture was in recession from 1927. **Dependence on the USA** • The German economy was heavily reliant on US loans and investment, leaving Germany vulnerable to US economic problems. **Problematic unemployment** • Unemployment did not fall below 1.3 million and levels were climbing before 1929. **Economic weaknesses** • The German economy did not perform as well as comparable economies, such as Britain and France. **Social tensions** • Tensions remained high between workers and business owners: industrial disputes were common and many industrialists resented the system of arbitration.

Spectrum of significance

Below are a sample Part (a) exam-style question and a list of general points which could be used to answer the question. Use your own knowledge and the information on the opposite page to reach a judgement about the extent to which each point suggests Weimar Germany experienced 'Golden Years' in the period 1924–1929. Write numbers on the spectrum below to indicate their relative importance. Having done this, write a brief justification of your placement, explaining why some of these factors are more important than others. The resulting diagram could form the basis of an essay plan.

How accurate is it to describe the period from 1923 to 1929 as the 'Golden Years' of the Weimar Republic?

1. The formation of the Grand Coalition in 1928
2. Hindenburg elected President in 1925
3. KPD gain 10.6 per cent of the vote in 1928
4. Between 1923 and 1929, seven governments were formed
5. By 1928, German economic output reached pre-war levels
6. Unemployment never fell below 1.3 million
7. Wages rose every year between 1924 and 1930

⟵⟶

Golden years   Years of turmoil

The flaw in the argument

Below are a sample Part (a) exam-style question and a paragraph written in answer to this question. The paragraph contains an argument, but there is a flaw in this argument. Use your knowledge of the topic to identify the flaw in the argument.

'Between 1924 and 1929, democracy in Germany was highly successful.' How far do you agree with this opinion?

Democracy in Germany was clearly highly successful in the period 1924 to 1929 because the Weimar regime was politically stable. There were seven consecutive governments formed between 1923 and 1929, including Müller's 'Grand Coalition'. The Grand Coalition was formed in 1928 and enjoyed over 60 per cent of the support from the Reichstag. Notably, other governments during this period had much smaller majorities and some enjoyed only a minority of support in the Reichstag. Support for extremist parties also grew towards the end of this period. For example, support for the KPD reached 10.6 per cent in 1928. Political co-operation in the Reichstag was often difficult. For example, radicals in the SPD found it difficult to co-operate with moderates in other parties. Consequently, Luther's 1926 coalition collapsed over the trivial issue of the appearance of the German flag. Democracy in Germany was highly successful during the 'Golden Years' of the Weimar Republic because of the political stability of the regime in these years.

1924–1929: 'Golden Years'– foreign policy and culture

Were the golden years really so golden?

Foreign policy

There were many positive developments in the arena of foreign policy in the period 1924–1929 as Germany was reconciled with the international community.

■ The Ruhr crisis ended: Stresemann's actions had ended the Ruhr crisis and France and Belgium left the Ruhr in 1925.

■ Reparations were renegotiated: as foreign minister, Stresemann pursued a policy of **fulfilment** of Germany's international obligations through payments of reparations. Fulfilment enabled Stresemann to renegotiate reparations and gain foreign loans and investment through the Dawes Plan of 1924 and the Young Plan of 1929.

■ In 1925, Stresemann agreed to Germany's post-war borders with France as part of the Locarno Pact.

■ Germany was admitted to the League of Nations in 1926.

The Young Plan, 1929

An international agreement easing the burden of reparations on Germany, the Young Plan increased the repayment term to 59 years and reduced annual repayments. The Young Plan was opposed by the nationalist right, however. A right-wing coalition, including the DNVP and the Nazis with some backing from nationalist industrialists like the steel magnate Fritz Thyssen, organised a referendum opposing the Young Plan. Their proposal only attracted the support of 13.9 per cent of people who voted.

Weimar culture and society in the 1920s

Newly democratic Germany saw a flourishing of cultural experimentation and a more liberal and tolerant atmosphere. Society also reflected these values: gay life flourished in Berlin, and some young women in cities were able to pursue careers and live in an independent manner. Many Germans did not regard these cultural changes positively, however, and came to associate the Weimar system with **decadence** and experimentation. Outside large urban areas, most Germans still preferred traditional culture and traditional roles for women, and did not tolerate homosexuality.

Weimar artistic culture

● In art, George Grosz and Otto Dix produced works reflecting on the impact of the First World War and satirising the *Junker* class.

● In architecture and design, the hugely influential **Bauhaus** movement created modern designs for buildings, furniture and graphics.

● In music, American jazz became very popular and began to influence the sound of German popular music. There was a lively jazz scene in Berlin.

● In literature, Erich Maria Remarque's *All Quiet on the Western Front* (1929) looked at the traumatic impact of the First World War on German soldiers.

● In cinema, Germany had a world-leading industry and **expressionist** works, such as Fritz Lang's *Metropolis* (1927), were particularly influential.

● Satirical forms of **Cabaret** were popular in Berlin.

Support or challenge?

Below is a sample Part (a) exam-style question which asks how far you agree with a specific statement. Below this is a series of general statements which are relevant to the question. Using your own knowledge and the information on the opposite page decide whether these statements support or challenge the statement in the question and tick the appropriate box.

How accurate is it to describe the period from 1924 to 1929 as the 'Golden Years' of the Weimar Republic?

	SUPPORT	CHALLENGE
Germany was admitted to the League of Nations in 1926.		
Urban culture was experimental and liberal.		
Stresemann pursued a policy of fulfilment.		
Many Germans believed that Weimar culture was decadent.		
The Young Plan was agreed in 1929.		
A far-right referendum on the Young Plan failed.		
Rural culture was traditional and illiberal.		

Recommended reading

Below is a list of suggested further reading on this topic.

- *Weimar Germany: Promise and Tragedy*, pages 7–41, Eric D Weitz (2007)
- *The Weimar Republic,* pages 50–57, Stephen J Lee (1998)
- *Weimar Germany: The Republic of the Reasonable*, pages 145–59, Paul Bookbinder (1997)

Exam focus

Below is a sample A grade Part (a) essay. Read it and the examiner comments around it.

'By 1929, Weimar Germany was a stable democracy.' How far do you agree with this opinion?

The introduction makes a useful contrast between the superficial and the real stability of the Weimar regime. However, this argument is not continued throughout the essay.

The period 1924 to 1929 has often been referred to as Germany's 'Golden Years'. By 1929, it appeared that Weimar Germany was a stable democracy. However, there were fundamental political and economic weaknesses, such as the nature of the Weimar constitution and the reliance on foreign loans, which indicate that this stability was superficial, rather than real.

This paragraph deals with Stresemann's successes in both economics and foreign policy. Consequently, the paragraph shows a good range of knowledge.

Stresemann's reforms gave Weimar Germany a degree of stability. Stresemann improved Germany's domestic and international position in a variety of ways. For example, he began paying reparations again, meaning that French troops withdrew from the Ruhr. Stresemann also worked closely with banker and economist, Hjalmar Schacht to create a new currency (the Rentenmark) which was more secure as it was tied to Germany's industrial and agricultural assets. This ended hyperinflation. Moreover, Stresemann managed to negotiate the Dawes Plan of 1924, which reduced Germany's reparation payments to 1 million gold marks a year in the period 1924 to 1929. The combination of the Dawes Plan, the end of hyperinflation and the introduction of a new currency, led to years of general growth and affluence in Germany. For example, by 1928 national income was 12 per cent higher than in 1913 and wage rates increased every year from 1924 to 1930. Stresemann also improved Germany's international status by gaining the confidence of western powers, to the extent that Germany was allowed to join the League of Nations in 1926. Additionally, the Locarno Pact of 1925 stabilised Germany's relations with France by agreeing the borders between the two countries. In these ways Stresemann's reforms gave Weimar democracy a degree of stability as they resolved the economic crisis of 1923 and rebuilt relations with foreign powers.

Here, the candidate supports the point with statistics. This shows depth of knowledge.

Another point to suggest that by 1929 German democracy was stable is the idea that Weimar Germany had finally achieved political solidity. By 1928, extreme parties were polling less than a quarter of votes cast. Indeed, in the 1928 election, the Nazi Party won a mere 2.6 per cent of the vote in the Reichstag elections. Furthermore, the 'Grand Coalition' formed in 1928 under Hermann Müller, enjoyed 60 per cent support in the Reichstag during their period in office. Overall, law and order had been generally restored to Germany. This political stability led to wider support from German citizens. Weimar gained more support than it had in previous years, with the popularity of pro-Weimar parties reaching 76 per cent in 1928. Furthermore, it cannot be ignored that the Weimar government had always received support from Germany's working classes, because of its promise of a welfare state. Clearly, by 1929 there was a degree of political stability because the majority of the public and the Reichstag backed democracy.

One point to suggest that by 1929 Weimar Germany was not a stable democracy is the idea that the political system on which it was based was fundamentally flawed. The Weimar constitution, which entailed proportional representation, led to coalition governments. This meant it was very difficult for governments to stay together. Indeed there were seven different governments in Germany between 1923 and 1929, some of which did not command a majority of support in the Reichstag. Furthermore, the constitution left the army unreformed, still dominated by the old elite who were not committed to supporting the new democracy. The judiciary too were never brought under government control. Its judgments often represented a conservative bias. For example, 354 murders by right-wing political groups led to only one life sentence. Finally, the constitution was largely based on liberal beliefs, meaning it had little scope for public censorship, allowing left- and right-wing threats to re-emerge at any point. In this way, Weimar Germany was not a stable democracy because its constitution did not allow for strong or decisive governments to rule Germany, and as the constitution allowed powerful institutions, such as the army and the judiciary, to undermine democratic values.

Another point to suggest that democracy in Weimar Germany was not stable is the instability of the economic recovery. For example, unemployment never fell below 1.3 million and from 1927, agriculture was in recession. Germany had been disadvantaged by the loss of resources, from areas such as Alsace Lorraine, which were returned to France in the Treaty of Versailles. Overall, the German economy became over-reliant on foreign loans, in particular the loans from the USA which totalled 25.5 billion marks from 1924 to 1930. Consequently, Germany suffered alongside America following the Wall Street Crash of 1929. Democracy in Weimar Germany was not therefore completely stable, as popular support for the government depended on the country's economic success, which in turn depended on the success of foreign economies.

In conclusion, Weimar Germany was not really a stable democracy because, although Stresemann created a degree of economic growth, this was largely based on American loans — an insecure foundation. Equally, although there was some political stability, the constitutional position of the army and the right-wing bias of the judiciary were threats to the long-term stability of Weimar democracy.

This paragraph begins to introduce balance to the essay by considering ways in which Weimar Germany was not a stable democracy.

The paragraph finishes with a clear analytical link to the question, explaining why Germany's economic situation undermined its political stability.

The conclusion presents a focused summary of the essay. However, it too fails to develop the argument mentioned in the introduction.

24/30

This essay is awarded a mark in Level 4 as it focuses clearly on the question, provides detailed examples to support its points, and links back to the question with an analytical statement at the end of each paragraph. However, the essay cannot be awarded a mark within Level 5 because it does not contain sustained analysis. Although an argument is stated in the introduction, this is not continued throughout the essay.

Moving from Level 4 to Level 5

The Exam Focus at the end of Section 1 provided a Level 5 essay. The essay here achieves a Level 4. Read both essays, and the examiner's comments provided. Make a list of the additional features required to push a Level 4 essay into Level 5.

Section 4: The rise of the Nazis

Hitler did not overthrow the Weimar Republic. Rather, he was appointed as Chancellor in January 1933. The factors that enabled this to happen are complex. To start to understand the circumstances of Hitler's and the Nazis' rise to power we will first examine the origins and ideas of the party.

Origins

The German Workers' Party (DAP) was founded by Anton Drexler in politically unstable Munich in the aftermath of the First World War. Despite the party's socialist-sounding name, Drexler hoped to attract German workers away from support for **socialism** and communism and towards support for a nationalist agenda by addressing some of their concerns.

Adolf Hitler, an Austrian national who had served in the German army during the First World War, was sent by the German army to report upon the DAP's activities. At this time, the party was very small and had very little impact but, interested in the DAP's stance, Hitler joined and soon made an impact through his powerful **oratory** in speeches that condemned the **Treaty of Versailles** and communists and blamed Jews for Germany's problems. The party was now renamed the National Socialist German Workers' Party (or NSDAP, commonly referred to as the Nazis). In 1920, Drexler and Hitler drew up the party programme, the 25 Points, and in 1921 Hitler became leader, or Führer, of the party.

Ideas

The 25 Points contained the key elements of the Nazi Party message. Hitler developed this ideology in speeches and his books *Mein Kampf* (1925) and *Zweites Buch* (1928).

His main ideas were:

- **German nationalism**: Germany should be strong, and all German-speaking peoples should be united in order to help maximise German strength. To develop German power, colonial expansion into Eastern Europe was needed. This 'living space' was called **Lebensraum**. In order for Germany to be strong, the Treaty of Versailles should be repudiated.

- **Racial ideas**: at the core of Hitler's ideas were false notions about race. These ideas had their origins in pseudo-scientific notions of the day. Hitler believed that differences between racial groups were profound and significant. Furthermore, he thought that races were organised into a hierarchy with Aryans, a Germanic-Nordic race, at the top. As a German nationalist, Hitler wanted Germany to maximise its strength, something he thought was only possible if a racially pure Aryan society was created in Germany. In his view racial purity equalled national strength.

- **Anti-Semitism**: Hitler believed Jews to be a race and developed the notion that Aryan strength would be compromised and polluted through interbreeding with Jews, whom he regarded as a vastly inferior racial group. Hitler also believed that Jews were engaged in a plot to sap Aryan racial strength through interbreeding.

- **Social Darwinism**: Hitler also subscribed to Social Darwinist ideas. The notion of the 'survival of the fittest' was used as a moral principle by Hitler who believed that not only did the fittest or strongest of species survive, but that it was morally right that the strongest triumph. Thus 'weaker' races and people should be eradicated.

Fascism

The philosophy of Hitler and the Nazis was fascism. Fascism combines a usually racist nationalism with militarism and belief in a strong state and strong authoritarian leadership. Fascism is anti-democratic and anti-socialist.

Complete the Venn diagram

Use the information on the opposite page to add detail to the Venn diagram below. In the non-intersecting areas of the diagram, list aspects of Nazi ideology relating only to nationalism, racism (including anti-Semitism) or Social Darwinism. In the intersecting areas of the diagram, note ways in which these ideologies overlapped.

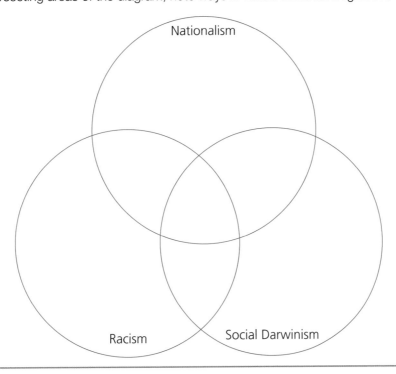

Nationalism

Racism   Social Darwinism

 Eliminate irrelevance (a)

Below are a sample Part (a) exam-style question and a paragraph written in answer to this question. Read the paragraph and identify parts of the paragraph that are not directly relevant to the question. Draw a line through the information that is irrelevant and justify your deletions in the margin.

To what extent was Nazi ideology the main reason for the success of the Nazi movement in the period 1929 to 1932?

One of the reasons for the success of the Nazi movement in the period 1929 to 1932 was Nazi ideology. German nationalism appealed to many German people in the wake of the Wall Street Crash, which was not the cause of the Great Depression, but was a catalyst, and also following Germany's humiliating defeat in the First World War. Nazi nationalism asserted that Germany should be strong, and that all German-speaking peoples should be united in one state. Nazi nationalism also repudiated the terms of the Treaty of Versailles. The Treaty of Versailles was given this name because it was signed in the Palace of Versailles, in France. Social Darwinism, the notion that the fittest survive, implied that stronger races would inevitably dominate weaker races. Combined with German nationalism, these racist ideas gave hope to many Germans that the humiliation of the 1920s would be replaced inevitably by a strong Germany that would dominate Europe. Social Darwinism should not be confused with the theories of Charles Darwin, an English naturalist. Nazi ideology was one reason for the success of the Nazi movement because it promised the rebirth of the German nation and Aryan race.

The early years of the party

Revised

The Munich Putsch, November 1923

In the early 1920s, Hitler cultivated links with the elite in Munich and started to build up support for the party. He worked with Ernst Röhm to develop an armed wing of the party, the **Sturmabteilung (SA)**. In the atmosphere of crisis in late 1923, Hitler attempted to take over the government. On 8 November in a beer hall in Munich, Hitler and Röhm, with the backing of ex-military leader General Ludendorff, took control of a conservative political meeting and Hitler announced a national revolution. Hitler hoped to unite right-wing nationalists in an armed march to seize control. In the event, some of the conservative politicians upon whose support Hitler had counted reported the plot to the authorities and the Bavarian police were able to stop the Putsch as its participants marched through Munich on 9 November.

Wilderness years

Following the Putsch, Hitler and other conspirators were put on trial. Despite the evident sympathy of the judge, Hitler was found guilty of **treason**. He only received a short sentence, however. After the Putsch, the Nazis were banned in Bavaria. With Hitler in jail and the party led by the ineffectual Alfred Rosenberg, the Nazis were weak and in disarray. Despite these problems, the Putsch did produce a number of benefits for Hitler:

- In prison, Hitler had the time to write *Mein Kampf*, or *My Struggle*. Sales of this book helped to support Hitler in his political work after his release.
- Hitler reconsidered his tactics following the Putsch, and decided to use the Weimar system to try to gain power not through force, but through electoral success.

Upon Hitler's release, he set about regaining a grip on the party and reorganising the party machine to increase its effectiveness:

- Hitler persuaded the Chancellor of Bavaria to lift the ban on the party in 1925.
- In 1925, a small bodyguard for Hitler led by Heinrich Himmler, the **Schutzstaffel (SS)**, was formed.
- At the **Bamberg Conference** in 1926, Hitler asserted his ideology and the *Führerprinzip*.
- Hitler also established a national party network during this time. Regional party bosses, called **gauleiters**, were appointed by and accountable to Hitler. This party structure assisted with election campaigning and the Nazi Party takeover.
- This era would also see the development of many of the party organisations that would later help the Nazis to target and involve various groups in German society: Nazi organisations were set up for doctors and teachers, and an agricultural movement was established in 1930 to try to draw in the peasantry.

Despite these efforts and the development of Nazi propaganda under Joseph Goebbels, the Nazi Party made very little impact in the 1928 election, gaining only 2.6 per cent of the vote. The better performance of the party in some rural areas, such as Schleswig-Holstein, did perhaps suggest that where people experienced economic hardship, as many were in the countryside, the Nazi message had some impact.

The *Führerprinzip*

The *Führerprinzip* was the principle that within the Nazi Party Hitler possessed all power and authority. It later became the operating principle for the Nazi state.

Spot the mistake

Below are a sample Part (a) exam-style question and a paragraph written in answer to this question. Why does this paragraph not get into Level 4? Once you have identified the mistake, rewrite the paragraph so that it displays the qualities of Level 4. The mark scheme on page 117 will help you.

> To what extent do you agree that Hitler's leadership was the main reason why the Nazis had emerged as a mass movement by 1932?

One reason why the Nazis had emerged as a mass movement by 1932 was Hitler's leadership. Hitler took a series of strategic decisions in the period 1924 to 1928 which established the foundation from which a mass movement grew. For example, after his release from prison in 1924, he reorganised the party, eliminating rivals such as Alfred Rosenberg. Additionally, at the Bamberg Conference of 1926, Hitler persuaded the party to accept the ideology of the Führerprinzip. This meant that Hitler was able to assert total dominance over the Nazi Party. Finally, Hitler established a national party network, controlled by gauleiters, who were directly accountable to Hitler.

Develop the detail

Below are a sample Part (a) exam-style question and a paragraph written in answer to this question. The paragraph contains a limited amount of detail. Annotate the paragraph to add additional detail to the answer.

> To what extent do you agree that Hitler's leadership was the main reason why the Nazis had emerged as a mass movement by 1932?

One reason why the Nazis had emerged as a mass movement by 1932 was that Hitler recruited a series of henchmen who helped to build the party. One of these henchmen was Ernst Röhm, who developed the SA who helped the growth of the party by attacking their political opponents. Röhm played a key role in the 1920s. Another of Hitler's henchmen was Joseph Goebbels. Goebbels was in charge of propaganda. Hitler's key henchmen were never a threat to his power. Thus, the Nazis emerged as a mass movement by 1932 because Hitler recruited talented henchmen, who furthered the appeal of the party and were loyal to the leader.

Economic and political crisis in Germany, 1929–1933

In 1928, the Nazi Party were a small party with minimal support. Yet only four years later they became the most popular party in Germany with more than 37 per cent of the vote in the July 1932 election. The economic and political crisis that Germany experienced made the Nazis and their message much more appealing.

The economic impact of the Depression

Following the **Wall Street Crash** in October 1929, the US economy experienced a severe depression. The German economy was heavily dependent upon US money and therefore greatly affected when US investment dried up and loans were recalled.

The German economy was severely affected:

- National income shrunk by 39 per cent between 1929 and 1932.
- Industrial production declined by more than 40 per cent.
- The number of unemployed rose to around 6 million by 1932. One-third of people of working age were out of work.
- Some 50,000 businesses were bankrupted.
- In 1931, as the German economy collapsed, a banking crisis was triggered and five major banks went bankrupt.
- Homelessness and poverty increased and people's standard of living decreased: many felt insecure and desperate.

The political impact of the Depression

The political system struggled to cope with these difficulties and parliamentary government declined:

- The **Grand Coalition** government led by Müller fell apart as the parties in government disagreed over the issue of unemployment benefits.
- Following the collapse of the Grand Coalition, subsequent governments were minority administrations which lacked Reichstag support. Chancellor Brüning's government failed to get backing for its budget in July 1930. Consequently

Hindenburg **dissolved** the Reichstag and called a new election. Chancellor von Papen's government lost a **vote of no-confidence** in 1932, while Chancellor von Schleicher's administration lasted for only two months.

Weimar Chancellors 1928–1933	
Hermann Müller	June 1928 – March 1930
Heinrich Brüning	March 1930 – May 1932
Franz von Papen	May 1932 – November 1932
Kurt von Schleicher	December 1932 – January 1933

- The German political system moved in a more authoritarian direction in the years before Hitler became Chancellor. Brüning and von Papen relied extensively on emergency presidential **decrees** rather than on parliamentary government: there were 44 emergency decrees issued under Article 48 in 1931 compared with just five in 1930, for example. In July 1932, von Papen and Hindenburg also used Article 48 to seize control of regional government in **Prussia**, still the largest and most populous German state, whose **left-wing SPD**-led government they objected to.
- Politicians did not take effective action to deal with the Depression. Modest reflationary measures were only started in mid-1932. German people lost faith in their political system as politicians failed to help them effectively: Brüning was labelled the 'hunger Chancellor'.
- Democratic norms broke down as political violence returned to the streets of Germany. During the July 1932 election campaign, there were 461 riots in Prussia in which a number of people died. The SA were responsible for much of the violence as they participated in battles against communists. Street violence added to an air of instability in Germany which served to increase people's discontent. Political and military leaders were aware that in practice Hitler was the only person capable of controlling the SA.

Simple essay style

Below is a sample Part (a) exam-style question. Use your own knowledge and the information on the opposite page to produce a plan for this question. Choose four general points, and provide three pieces of specific information to support each general point. Once you have planned your essay, write the introduction and conclusion for the essay. The introduction should list the points to be discussed in the essay. The conclusion should summarise the key points and justify which point was the most important.

'The impact of the Great Depression was the prime reason for the emergence of the Nazis as a mass movement between 1929 and 1932.' How far do you agree with this opinion?

Complete the paragraph

Below are a sample Part (a) exam-style question and a paragraph written in answer to this question. The paragraph contains a point and specific examples, but lacks a concluding explanatory link back to the question. Complete the paragraph, adding this link in the space provided.

'The failure of mainstream politicians in the period 1929–1932 led to the emergence of the Nazis as a mass movement.' How far do you agree with this view?

The failure of mainstream politicians during the Depression was clearly one reason why the Nazis had emerged as a mass movement by 1932. In the aftermath of the Depression, Müller's Grand Coalition fell apart. A combination of political weakness and constitutional difficulties led to the collapse of Müller's, then Brüning's, then von Papen's, then von Schleicher's governments. Brüning and von Papen attempted to restore order by governing through emergency presidential decrees. Indeed, 44 emergency decrees were issued in 1931 alone. However, mainstream politicians were unable to gain popular support and could not even govern with the full support of the Reichstag. Mainstream politicians also failed to restore economic growth. Brüning's economic schemes were far too small to bring about economic recovery.

_____

_____

The growth of Nazi support

The Depression and political crisis provided an opportunity for the Nazis. As the Depression hit, the party's electoral success increased dramatically, as did their membership, which was around 2 million by early 1933. Members were also attracted to Nazi Party organisations, such as the Hitler Youth and the SA.

The Nazis' new popularity put Hitler in contention for the chancellorship of Germany.

Nazi Party vote, Reichstag elections

Election date	1928	1930	July 1932*
Percentage of the vote	2.6%	18.3%	37.3%
Number of seats	12	107	230

*After these elections, the Nazi Party was the largest in the Reichstag.

The demographics of Nazi voters and Nazi members

- A much larger number of people voted for the Nazi Party than were members.
- Nazi members were most likely to be young (two-thirds of members in 1930 were aged under 40) and male, partly because the party did not encourage active female participation.
- However, women were more likely to vote for the party than men. Hitler had some success in appealing to traditionally minded women who had not previously voted.
- Catholics were less likely to support the Nazis than Protestants, as the majority of Catholic voters supported the Centre Party.
- Urban dwellers were less likely to vote for the Nazis.
- **Working-class** people formed the largest number of Nazi Party members at 31 per cent, but were on average less likely to be members of the party than most other social classes. This apparent paradox can be accounted for as, at 46 per cent, the working class formed the largest social group in Germany.
- Office workers and the self-employed or *Mittelstand* were over-represented as party members.

The impact of propaganda

Nazi propaganda was tailored to different audiences to try to maximise their support:

- Messages about bread and work were deployed in working-class areas.
- Messages about the Weimar Republic's supposedly lax moral standards were tailored to conservative mothers.
- **Anti-Semitic** messages were targeted at small shopkeepers.

The Nazis used posters, leaflets, rallies and speeches to disseminate their propaganda as well as modern technology, such as radio and film. Rallies were designed to provoke an emotional response through the orchestration of image, sound and emotive messages. The Nazis also benefited from their association with the DNVP as their leader, Alfred Hugenberg, put his media empire, consisting of various newspapers and radio stations, at the service of Nazi propagandists. The impact of propaganda was important, but it should be noted that the Nazis' vote increased dramatically even in areas where they did not target propaganda.

Hitler's appeal

Joseph Goebbels cultivated an image for Hitler as Germany's heroic saviour. At a time when politicians seemed weak and ineffective this image was very appealing. This 'Hitler Myth' helped to gain support for Hitler and the Nazis. During the presidential election of 1932, Hitler ran against President Hindenburg. Hitler's campaign 'Hitler over Germany' portrayed the Nazi leader as dynamic and modern as he harnessed modern technology to put his message across, and innovatively travelled via aeroplane to campaign. Hitler came second in the election and had established himself as a credible political leader.

Support or challenge?

Below is a sample Part (a) exam-style question which asks how far you agree with a specific statement. Below this is a series of general statements which are relevant to the question. Using your own knowledge and the information on the opposite page decide whether these statements support or challenge the statement in the question and tick the appropriate box.

'Hitler's leadership was primarily responsible for creating a mass Nazi movement in the period 1929 to 1932.' How far do you agree with this opinion?

	SUPPORT	CHALLENGE
Hitler was a good orator.		
National income shrank by 39% during the Depression.		
The Weimar constitution failed to ensure strong government.		
The Nazis failed to seize power in the Munich Putsch.		
The Nazi Party was disciplined by the *Führerprinzip*.		
Brüning and von Papen used Article 48 extensively between 1930 and 1932.		
Hitler published *Mein Kampf* in 1925.		
Under the Treaty of Versailles, Germany accepted responsibility for the First World War.		

Introducing an argument

Below are a sample Part (a) exam-style question, a list of key points to be made in the essay, and a simple introduction and conclusion for the essay. Read the question, the plan, and the introduction and conclusion. Rewrite the introduction and the conclusion in order to develop an argument.

Why did the Nazi Party become a mass movement in the years 1929 to 1932?

Key points

- Hitler's leadership
- The failure of mainstream politicians
- Economic crisis
- The appeal of Nazi ideology

Introduction

There were a number of key reasons why the Nazi Party became a mass movement in the years 1929 to 1932. These were Hitler's leadership, the failure of mainstream politicians, economic crisis and the appeal of Nazi ideology.

Conclusion

There were a number of key reasons why the Nazi Party became a mass movement in the years 1929 to 1932. The most important reason was Hitler's leadership. This played a more significant role than all of the other factors.

Support from the conservative elite

President Hindenburg resisted appointing Hitler after the July 1932 election, despite the Nazis' electoral success. Hindenburg offered him the vice-chancellorship, but Hitler refused, holding out for the chancellorship. Mass popularity was not sufficient for Hitler to be appointed. Rather, it was the support that he received from some in the political and economic elite that led to his appointment:

■ As the economic and political crisis continued, **conservatives** in big business and in the army turned to Hitler for fear of a communist takeover. The KPD had seen its vote increase from 3.2 million in 1928 to 5.9 million in November 1933. It was the Nazis' determination to smash the communist militia that caused conservatives to back Hitler.

  – Influential industrialists and bankers, including Hjalmar Schacht, IG Farben and Gustav Krupp, put pressure on Hindenburg to appoint Hitler Chancellor. They feared losing their wealth and power in the event of a communist takeover.

  – Army leaders told Hindenburg that they would be unable to deal with uprisings from both the communist militia and the SA. Therefore, they urged Hindenburg to do a deal with Hitler in order to gain the support of the SA.

■ Hitler benefited from von Papen's schemes against Chancellor von Schleicher, appointed in December 1932. Von Papen and others around him such as Hindenburg's son Oscar and his state secretary, Otto Meissner, worked to persuade Hindenburg to appoint Hitler as Chancellor. Von Papen's plan involved his own appointment as vice Chancellor: Nazi members of the Cabinet were to be a minority. Von Papen wanted to use Hitler's popular support to give the legitimacy to an authoritarian government that his own government had lacked in 1932. Von Papen assumed that he would be able to control Hitler.

■ Many members of the conservative political and economic elite contributed to the Nazis' funds, including Hugenberg and steel manufacturer Fritz Thyssen.

■ Hindenburg eventually appointed Hitler after von Schleicher's plan to gain an element of popular legitimacy for his government by working with part of the Nazi movement and the trade unions collapsed. Von Papen's government had completely failed to gain Reichstag support, and now so did von Schleicher's.

■ Hindenburg at this point finally relented and appointed Hitler: despite a decline in the Nazis' vote share in the November 1932 election (from around 37 per cent to 32 per cent), the party was still the largest in the Reichstag.

> **German conservatives**
>
> German conservatives were from the old **Junker** elite or the new business class. They had in common with the fascist Nazis a hatred for socialists and communists, nationalist leanings and a desire for more authoritarian government.

Hitler's appointment to power

On 30 January 1933, Hitler was appointed as Chancellor of Germany, with von Papen as Vice Chancellor in a cabinet that only contained two other Nazi members.

Factors in Hitler's appointment to power

The economic depression and the failure of politicians to deal with it effectively gave Hitler an opportunity, as more people listened to his message. Many were profoundly disillusioned with Weimar democracy, which was not strongly **entrenched** and which, in any case, never appeared to have worked very effectively. The Nazis saw their support rise dramatically between 1929 and 1932, until they were the most popular political party. Supported by some conservatives who saw the Nazis as a means to create a populist authoritarian government, Hindenburg was eventually persuaded to appoint Hitler as Chancellor.

Other factors contributing to Hitler's appointment to power include: Hitler's personal role (as a charismatic leader and tactician); the impact of Nazi propaganda; and SA violence.

RAG – Rate the timeline

Below are a sample Part (a) exam-style question and a timeline. Read the question, study the timeline and, using three coloured pens, put a Red, Amber or Green star next to the events to show:

Red: Events and policies that have no relevance to the question
Amber: Events and policies that have some significance to the question
Green: Events and policies that are directly relevant to the question

1) Why did the Nazi Party become a mass movement in the years 1929 to 1932?

Now repeat the activity with the following questions:

2) To what extent was the success of Weimar democracy during the 'Golden Years' the main reason why the Nazi Party were unable to become a mass movement prior to 1928?

3) How far do you agree that, by 1929, the Nazis had become a mass movement?

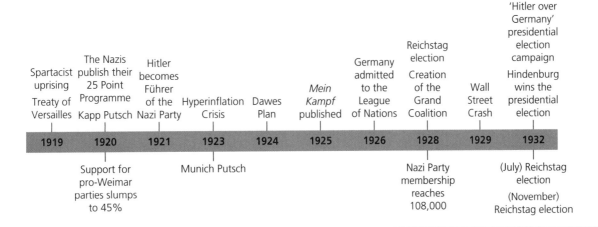

Spectrum of significance

Below are a sample Part (a) exam-style question and a list of general points which could be used to answer the question. Use your own knowledge and the information on the opposite page to reach a judgement about the importance of these general points to the question posed. Write numbers on the spectrum below to indicate their relative importance. Having done this, write a brief justification of your placement, explaining why some of these factors are more important than others. The resulting diagram could form the basis of an essay plan.

'Hitler became Chancellor in January 1933 due to the failure of Weimar democracy.' How far do you agree with this opinion?

1. The failure of Weimar democracy
2. The support of the conservative elites
3. The appeal of Hitler
4. The Great Depression
5. The failure of mainstream Weimar politicians
6. Nazi ideology

Very important   Less important

Nazi consolidation of power

When Hitler was appointed Chancellor, he had to overcome a series of obstacles in order to become dictator. Only three of the twelve Cabinet members were Nazis and President Hindenburg and the Reichstag retained their powers. However, by March 1933, Hitler had removed many of his political opponents, ended democracy and established a dictatorship. A number of events helped Hitler to strengthen his position.

The Reichstag Fire, 27 February 1933

A Dutch communist, Marinus van der Lubbe, is believed to have set fire to the Reichstag building. The Nazis claimed that the fire was part of a communist conspiracy. Some have argued that the Nazis staged the fire in order to create an impression of a communist conspiracy, but most historians now believe that van der Lubbe acted alone. President Hindenburg declared a national emergency in response to the fire and the supposed communist plot.

The Reichstag Fire Decree and the campaign against the left, 28 February 1933

In the days after the fire, President Hindenburg issued a decree (the Law for the Protection of People and State, or Reichstag Fire Decree), which suspended the parts of the Weimar constitution that included civil rights:

- German people and political organisations lost the right to free speech, a free press and the right to freedom of association.
- The right of **habeas corpus** was removed: the police and secret police now had the right to arrest people for any reason or none and people could be held indefinitely in captivity, something that was euphemistically called '**protective custody**'.
- There were mass arrests and widespread attacks on communists and some socialists and trade unionists.

Elections, 5 March 1933

The Reichstag elections of March 1933 were conducted in an atmosphere of violence and intimidation. The result was an increased vote share for the Nazis (43.5 per cent) and a Reichstag majority for them and their conservative supporters. This gave Hitler's government apparent legitimacy. But the election result cannot be considered as free or fair, as the SA harassed and attacked the KPD and SPD. Many members of the KPD had been arrested before the election.

Dachau opened, 20 March 1933

Dachau, near Munich, was the first **concentration camp**, and the Nazis' political opponents were imprisoned there.

Potsdam Day, 21 March 1933

Following the success of the Nazis and the conservatives in the Reichstag elections, a propagandistic 'day of national unity' was held at Potsdam, seat of the Kings of Prussia and Kaisers of Germany. Hindenburg and Hitler appeared before huge crowds together, to send out a message of Nazi and conservative unity. This helped to legitimise Nazi rule.

The Enabling Act, 24 March 1933

Hitler now moved to take dictatorial powers. He urged members of the Reichstag to pass an 'Enabling Act' to give him the power to issue law by decree, bypassing both the Reichstag and the President. Hitler had Hindenburg and von Papen's support: von Papen had envisaged that an authoritarian leader would be needed to act decisively to defeat the political left. A two-thirds majority in the Reichstag was needed for the Enabling Act to be passed. This was achieved, as the Centre Party were persuaded to back the Act, which was passed by 444 votes to 94. SPD members, some of whom were prevented from attending the vote by SA intimidation, were the only deputies to oppose the Enabling Act; members of the KPD were banned from attending.

The flaw in the argument (a)

Below are a sample Part (a) exam-style question and a paragraph written in answer to this question. The paragraph contains an argument, but there is a flaw in this argument. Use your knowledge of this topic to identify the flaw in the argument.

'Nazi consolidation of power in 1933 was primarily due to their use of violence and terror.' How far do you agree with this opinion?

The main way in which Hitler was able to consolidate Nazi power in 1933 was through the use of the Enabling Act. The passing of the Enabling Act in March 1933 effectively gave Hitler dictatorial powers. Consequently, he was able to open Dachau, a concentration camp outside Munich, where the Nazis' political prisoners were held in 'protective custody'. The Enabling Act also gave Hitler the power to suspend civil rights, removing the free press, the right to free speech, and the right to freedom of association, the first step towards the creation of a single-party state. The Enabling Act also gave Hitler the power to harass and attack the SPD and the KPD during the March 1933 elections. Political violence during these elections enabled the Nazis to win a record 43.5 per cent of the popular vote. In this way, the Enabling Act was the main reason for the Nazi consolidation of power because it allowed Hitler to gain dictatorial power by imprisoning his opponents, rigging elections and suspending civil rights.

Recommended reading

Below is a list of suggested further reading on this topic.

- *The Face of the Third Reich*, pages 53–69, Joachim C Fest (1970)
- *From Kaiser to Führer: Germany 1900–45*, pages 193–205, Geoff Layton (2009)
- *Fascism: A History*, pages 110–13, Roger Eatwell (1995)

Factors enabling Nazi consolidation of power

Terror

The Nazis were partly able to consolidate their power because the Reichstag Fire Decree removed people's civil rights. Consequently, the elections of March 1933 were characterised by Nazi violence. The Enabling Act gave Hitler the power to eliminate opposition by establishing a one-party state. In 1933, the political left of Germany was smashed:

- Some 150,000–200,000 political opponents of the Nazi Party were imprisoned in 1933.
- **Concentration camps** were opened.
- The KPD was banned shortly after the Reichstag Fire, trade unions all shut on 1 May 1933, the SPD was banned in June 1933, and all other political parties disbanded by July 1933.
- Hundreds of left-wing newspapers were closed.

In July 1934, Hitler had a number of political opponents murdered (including conservatives like von Schleicher) and supporters whom he believed to be a threat, such as Ernst Röhm of the SA on the **Night of the Long Knives**.

The support of the conservative elite

Hitler and the Nazis were only able to consolidate their power because the conservatives they shared power with allowed them to do so:

- Hindenburg issued the Reichstag Fire Decree and von Papen and Hindenburg supported the Enabling Act, as did all conservative parties in the Reichstag.
- The Nazis were able to launch attacks on the political left partly because of the positions within the Cabinet that they had been given. Frick, at the Ministry of the Interior, was in charge of the security apparatus for the state, while Goering, who was Interior Minister for Prussia, was able to direct terror against the left in Prussia.
- The conservatives did not unwittingly give these powerful positions to the Nazis: von Papen wished to use the Nazis to crush the left and create authoritarian rule.

- Support from the conservative elite also came from some leading industrialists who bankrolled the Nazis during the March 1933 election. They promised the party 3 million Reich **marks** on 20 February 1933.

Propaganda

Goebbels' propaganda portrayed the government's actions as necessary to deal with a national emergency. Potsdam Day, which featured not just Hindenburg and Hitler, but also many generals, was an orchestrated piece of propaganda, aimed at demonstrating the unity and popularity of the government and the acceptance of the Nazis by traditional conservative elements.

An illusion of moderation

- The Reichstag Fire Decree and Enabling Act gave a veneer of pseudo legality to the Nazis' actions. Therefore, the Nazis were able to describe their consolidation of power as the 'legal revolution'.
- At first, Hitler was keen to appear moderate and emphasised national unity in his rhetoric.
- The **Concordat** with the Catholic Church of 20 July 1933 was designed to reassure Catholics, by protecting their religious freedoms in return for an agreement from the Church to stay out of political matters.

Gleichschaltung

The Nazis also consolidated power through a process of *Gleichschaltung*, or co-ordination, or more accurately, **Nazification**. The Law for the Restoration of Professional Civil Service of 7 April 1933 removed Jews and political opponents of the Nazis from the civil service, schools and courts. After independent trade unions were abolished, a Nazi labour organisation, the *Deutsche Arbeitsfront* (DAF) was established. The Nazis also moved to take over local government: regional parliaments were dissolved in March 1933 and Reich governors (usually Gauleiters) took over.

RAG – Rate the timeline

Below are a sample Part (a) exam-style question and a timeline. Read the question, study the timeline and, using three coloured pens, put a Red, Amber or Green star next to the events to show:

Red: Events and policies that have no relevance to the question
Amber: Events and policies that have some significance to the question
Green: Events and policies that are directly relevant to the question

1) 'Nazi consolidation of power in 1933 was primarily due to their use of violence and terror.' How far do you agree with this opinion?

Now repeat the activity with the following question:

2) Why were the Nazis able to consolidate their power so swiftly in the period January to July 1933?

Nov 1932	Jan	Feb	Mar	Apr	Jun	Jul	Jun 1934
Reichstag election: Nazi share of the vote declines to 32%	Hitler appointed as Chancellor	Reichstag Fire	Reichstag election: Nazis gain 43.5% of the vote	Law for the Restoration of the Professional Civil Service	SPD banned	All political parties, except for the Nazis, disbanded	Night of the Long Knives
Nov		Feb	Mar			Jul	
Von Schleicher appointed Chancellor		Law for the Protection of People and State	Dachau opened Potsdam Day Enabling Act			Concordat agreed with the Roman Catholic Church	

Developing an argument

Below are a sample Part (a) exam-style question, a list of key points to be made in the essay, and a paragraph from the essay. Read the question, the plan, and the sample paragraph. Rewrite the paragraph in order to develop an argument. Your paragraph should explain why the factor discussed in the paragraph is either the most significant factor or less significant than another factor.

To what extent was the support of the elites the main reason why the Nazis were able to consolidate their power in the period January to July 1933?

Key points:

- Support of the elites
- Violence and terror
- Propaganda
- The appearance of legality
- *Gleichschaltung*

Sample paragraph

The appearance of legality was one reason why the Nazis were able to consolidate their power in the period January to July 1933. For example, following the Reichstag Fire in February 1933, the Nazis used Article 48 of the constitution to issue a decree suspending civil rights. The decree took away the right to free speech, the freedom of the press, the right to freedom of association, and habeas corpus. As a result, Hitler was able to arrest trade unionists, communists and socialists, and claim that he had done so legally. The second aspect of the 'legal revolution' was the Enabling Act of March 1933. This gave Hitler freedom of action, independent of the Reichstag and the President. The Enabling Act allowed Hitler to ban both the SPD and the KPD, again claiming that this action was legal. In this way, the 'legal revolution' played a role in the Nazi consolidation of power because the suspension of civil rights and the passing of the Enabling Act allowed Hitler to create a dictatorship.

Exam focus

Below is a sample A grade Part (a) essay. Read it and the examiner comments around it.

To what extent was the popularity of the Nazi Party the main reason for Hitler's appointment as Chancellor in January 1933?

The introduction sets out an argument that will be pursued throughout the whole of the essay. In addition, it makes reference to all of the factors that will be discussed in the essay.

The popularity of the Nazi Party certainly played a role in Hitler's appointment as Chancellor. The party's popularity was attractive to the existing elites, who wanted to tie a strong government to a wide popular support base. Nonetheless, the Nazi Party had been popular for some time and yet Hindenburg had resisted pressure to appoint Hitler as Chancellor. The pressure from businessmen, mainstream politicians, such as von Papen, and the army was the decisive factor that persuaded Hindenburg to use his power as President to appoint Hitler as Chancellor. Other long-term factors which influenced the decision were the economic crisis, the weaknesses of the Weimar constitution, and Hitler's personal popularity.

The first paragraph deals with the factor stated in the question. Consequently, it answers the question set immediately.

By 1932, the Nazis were undoubtedly the most popular party in Germany. The July 1932 elections gave the Nazis 37.3 per cent of the popular vote and, with 230 seats, they became the largest party in the Reichstag. The Nazis appealed to young people, to men, to people living in rural areas, and even to a large number of working-class people. Even so, Nazi popularity on its own does not explain Hitler's appointment as Chancellor. Indeed, the Nazi victory in the July 1932 elections did not lead to an immediate offer of power. According to the Weimar constitution, the President could appoint a Chancellor independent of the popular vote or the size of a party in the Reichstag. In 1932, Hindenburg was concerned about SA violence, and had personal reservations about Hitler's suitability to lead the government. He was not swayed by the Nazis' victory in the July 1932 election, and only appointed Hitler Chancellor six months later. Nazi popularity was not therefore the decisive factor that led to Hitler's appointment as Chancellor, as, on its own, it did not persuade Hindenburg that Hitler was the right man for the job.

Here, the candidate explains why this second factor is more important than the factor stated in the question. Crucially, the relative importance of the two factors is analysed, rather than simply asserted.

Hitler's appointment as Chancellor in January 1933 was largely due to pressure from the conservative elites. For example, Hjalmar Schacht, Gustav Krupp and industrialists representing IG Farben put pressure on Hindenburg to appoint Hitler as Chancellor. They feared a communist takeover and believed that the Nazis were the only party capable of preventing this from happening. Von Papen also lobbied for Hitler to be appointed Chancellor. He assumed that with Hindenburg as President, and himself as vice-Chancellor, the traditional elites would be able to control the government while harnessing popular support for the Nazis in order to stabilise the government. Finally, the army sided with Schacht and persuaded Hindenburg that the Nazis needed to be incorporated into the government as the army could not deal with a civil war between the communists and the SA. In this way, pressure from the conservative elite was the key factor in Hitler's appointment as Chancellor, because the conservatives were able to persuade Hindenburg to ignore his concerns about Hitler and appoint him as head of government. Nonetheless, popularity still played an important role as the conservative elite wanted to consolidate their power by utilising the popular support that the Nazis had generated since 1930.

Nazi popularity was a result of Germany's economic crisis. In 1928, at the end of Weimar's 'Golden Years', the Nazis received only 2.6 per cent of the popular vote. As the economic crisis deepened following the Wall Street Crash, Nazi popularity rose to 18.3 per cent in 1930, and 37.3 per cent in 1932. Between 1928 and 1933, there was a succession of short-lived, weak governments, under Brüning, von Papen, and von Schleicher. Brüning attempted small-scale schemes to revive the economy. However, these failed and Weimar's democratic culture broke down, leading to political violence and a rise in extremist politics. In this way, the economic crisis led to increased Nazi popularity because mainstream political parties were unable to deal with the crisis and therefore people looked for alternatives on the extreme left and extreme right. This in turn led the political elite to turn to Hitler, as they were unable to control the increasingly violent situation and as they feared a communist takeover.

> The candidate uses detailed statistics to support their argument, showing depth of knowledge.

Hitler's personal appeal was another important factor in his appointment as Chancellor. Joseph Goebbels masterminded Hitler's presidential election campaign of 1932. The campaign, 'Hitler over Germany', portrayed Hitler as a dynamic, modern and innovative leader. In the atmosphere of economic and political crisis, Hitler's image as a strong leader was extremely appealing to the German public. The traditional elites were not taken in by Hitler's propaganda, but they were forced to recognise that by mid-1932, Hitler was the leader of the most popular party in Germany, and, after Hindenburg, the most popular politician. The elites were also aware that Hitler was the only person who could control the SA. Fearing communist revolution or an SA putsch, the elites persuaded Hindenburg to appoint Hitler as Chancellor, and in so doing, use Nazi support to create a stronger, more authoritarian German state.

> Here, the candidate links all of the factors. This shows sustained analysis, and a comprehensive grasp of the topic.

In conclusion, the immediate cause of Hitler's appointment as Chancellor was the pressure put on Hindenburg by Germany's political elite. Nonetheless, the popularity of the Nazis also played a role as it persuaded the elites that Hitler was the only viable option as Chancellor. The economic and political crisis, and the failure of existing political leaders to deal with the trouble facing Germany heightened Hitler's popularity and persuaded the elites that an alliance with the Nazis was the only way to ensure a popular, authoritarian government with the strength to deal with Germany's problems.

> The conclusion weighs the relative significance of the different factors, and reflects the argument stated in the introduction and sustained throughout the essay.

30/30

This essay gains maximum marks because it contains sustained analysis supported by a good range of factors, developed in a large amount of detail. The essay creates sustained analysis by linking all of the factors that it discusses and showing their relative significance for Hitler's appointment as Chancellor.

Linking factors

One of the reasons why this essay is so successful is that it draws links between the factors it discusses. Read through the essay again, and highlight the points at which the factors are linked. Below is another example of an exam question. Draw a plan for your answer to this question. Annotate your plan to show how you would link the different factors discussed in the essay.

> 'Nazi consolidation of power in 1933 was primarily due to the miscalculations of the existing elites.' How far do you agree with this opinion?

Section 5: How popular and efficient was the Nazi regime in the years 1933–1939?

A consensus dictatorship?

Revised

There is considerable historical debate concerning whether the Nazi regime was one based on popular support (a consensus dictatorship) or whether, in fact, the Nazis' power rested on repression and terror.

Evidence that the regime was popular

The plebiscites

A series of **plebiscites** were held in Nazi Germany on various issues. The results of these tend to indicate that people supported Hitler's policies. Furthermore, these **referenda** helped to create a climate of what historian Ian Kershaw has called 'plebiscitary acclamation': Hitler regularly renewed his '**mandate**' to rule by holding referenda in which his policies would receive overwhelming support, thus giving the appearance that his regime was legitimate and popular.

Date	Plebiscite question	% in favour
1933	Do you agree with the government's decision to pull out of the **League of Nations**?	95%
1934	Do you endorse Hitler taking over Hindenburg's remaining powers on Hindenburg's death?	90%
1935	Do you want the Saarland to reunify with the rest of Germany?*	90%
1936	Do you support the remilitarisation of the Rhineland?	99%
1938	Do you support the union of Germany and Austria (**Anschluss**)?	99%

*The Saarland had been placed temporarily under League of Nations control after the First World War. In the Saarland itself, the League ran the plebiscite and results were similar to the result in the rest of Germany in the plebiscite that had been run by the Nazis.

Lack of opposition

Another argument that has been made to advance the idea that people supported the Nazi regime during the 1930s is that there was very little overt opposition to the regime during this time. There were no significant attempts to overthrow the regime, and the plots that there were against Hitler came from lone individuals, like Georg Elser, or groups in the elite, such as a plan to remove Hitler orchestrated by General Beck in 1938. These plots cannot be said to represent public opinion. In addition, underground opposition did not have widespread support during this era. Opposition groups tended to have only a small number of supporters.

Collaboration

Historian Robert Gellately has argued that the regime was a 'consensus dictatorship' because it relied so heavily on collaboration from ordinary people who were supportive of the Nazi regime. In his work *The Gestapo and German Society* (1990), Gellately found that in the city of Würzburg:

- There was not an extensive network of terror, as only 21 **Gestapo** officers covered the Würzburg area: Gestapo officers were overstretched.
- These officers did not have time to mount surveillance against lots of people, and relied heavily on denunciations from ordinary people in order to root out those who did not conform to the regime's ideals.

The support of ordinary Germans may suggest that people believed in Nazi ideas and wanted to work for the Nazis, or at least that people tolerated the Nazis and Nazi persecution of minority groups.

It can also be argued that the repression was not as extensive as is sometimes thought, with only 4000 people (mostly **a-socials**) held in **concentration camps** in 1935; the use of concentration camps seems to have been widely known about and supported by many German people in the 1930s.

Below are a sample Part (b) exam-style question and the three sources referred to in the question. In one colour, draw links between the sources to show ways in which they agree about the popularity of the Nazi regime. In another colour, draw links between the sources to show ways in which they disagree.

Use Sources 1, 2 and 3 and your own knowledge.

To what extent do you agree with the view that the Nazi regime rested on 'a good deal of consensus' between 1933 and 1939?

SOURCE 1

(From Ian Kershaw in The Hitler Myth, *published 1987)*

Few, if any, twentieth-century political leaders have enjoyed greater popularity among their own people than Hitler in the decade or so following his assumption of power on 30 January 1933. It has been suggested that at the peak of his popularity, nine Germans in ten were 'Hitler supporters, Führer believers.' … Acclaim for Hitler went way beyond acclaim for other leading Nazis, embracing many who were critical of the institutions, policies, and ideology of the regime.

The adulation of Hitler by millions of Germans who might otherwise have been only marginally committed to Nazism meant that the person of the Führer, as the focal point of basic consensus, formed a critical integratory force in the Nazi system of rule. Without Hitler's massive personal popularity, the high level of plebiscitary acclamation which the regime could repeatedly call upon – legitimating its actions at home and abroad, diffusing opposition, boosting the autonomy of the leadership from the traditional national-conservative elites who had imagined that they would keep Hitler in check – Nazi rule is unthinkable.

SOURCE 2

(From Richard J Evans in The Third Reich in Power, 1933–1939, *published 2005)*

The Gestapo quickly attained an almost mythical status as an all-seeing, all-knowing arm of state security and law enforcement. People soon began to suspect that it had agents in every pub and club, spies in every workplace or factory, informers lurking in every bus and tram and standing on every street corner. The reality was very different. The Gestapo was a very small organisation with a tiny number of paid agents and informers.

Fewer than 10 per cent of the cases with which the Gestapo dealt came from investigations it had begun itself. Most frequently, information on labour movement resistance activities came from Communists or Social Democrats whose will had been broken by torture and who had agreed to inform on their former comrades.

SOURCE 3

(From Robert Gellately in The Gestapo and German Society, *published 1990)*

In their efforts to uncover popular forms of resistance, historians have frequently lost sight of the broad field of consensus. [However], the German government could not have carried on for very long without a good deal of consensus, whether forced or passive, of a broad section of the population. . . . [Clearly], the Gestapo, and, by extension, the regime, could not have enforced racial policy on its own.

The ability of the regime to carry on . . . was not seriously affected by the existence and persistence of dissent, which flared into opposition on rare occasions.

A consensus dictatorship?

There is evidence that some aspects of the Nazi regime were genuinely popular.

The legacy of the Weimar Republic

One reason why people supported the Nazi regime was the perception that Weimar democracy had failed. People's memories of the political and economic crisis that characterised the final years of Weimar would be likely to increase support for a regime that seemed to bring greater stability to the lives of many Germans.

Popular policies?

Some of the regime's policies were genuinely popular and some of their policies did improve the lives of some Germans. In areas such as the economy and foreign policy, Nazi policy appeared successful:

- Unemployment reduced, falling to 1 million by January 1935, and economic growth returned.
- **Strength Through Joy** allowed some **working-class** people to enjoy more leisure activities. For example, 28,500 workers for Siemens in Berlin were able to take a holiday due to the programme.
- In foreign policy, the army managed to peacefully and successfully remilitarise the Rhineland in 1936 and unify Germany with Austria in 1938.
- Evidence from reports produced by **SOPADE**, the **SPD** in exile, indicates that people viewed these areas of Nazi policy positively.

Some Nazi social policies also improved the standard of living for certain groups of people. Pregnant 'Aryan' women were given free health care and, by 1938, 2.5 million families benefited from increased benefits for larger families.

The impact of propaganda

Another reason why the Nazi regime might have been popular is that their propaganda was effective.

A Ministry of Popular Enlightenment and Propaganda led by Joseph Goebbels was established in 1933 and promoted propaganda in various ways:

- Newspaper editors were essentially censored as they were accountable to the Propaganda Ministry for what they published.
- Newspapers also received daily press briefings.
- The content of **newsreels** was controlled.
- Radio was used to propagate Nazi messages.
- The annual Nazi Party Nuremberg Rally became a showcase for Nazi power.
- Education and Nazi organisations like the Hitler Youth and the Nazi Women's League were also used to promote Nazi ideas.

It should be noted, however, that, whilst propaganda could help to account for the level of support for the Nazi state, it does undermine the argument that the state was a 'consensus dictatorship', as if people were subject to propaganda they may have been manipulated into supporting the regime, and cannot be said to have *freely* consented.

Furthermore, the impact of propaganda should not be overestimated: propaganda was most effective when it built upon people's existing ideas or prejudices. It did not succeed in creating a nation unified around a Nazi *Volksgemeinschaft*.

The Hitler Myth

Goebbels worked hard to create an image of Hitler as a saviour of Germany. Hitler was shown in poses reminiscent of Jesus or as a modern day **Teutonic Knight**. The Hitler Myth associated Hitler with the popular aspects of the regime, such as foreign policy and the 1936 Olympics. It presented Hitler as a representative of the whole nation who stood above politics. The positive view that many people had of Hitler contributed to the level of support that the Nazi regime enjoyed in the 1930s.

Below are a sample Part (b) exam-style question and the three sources referred to in the question. In one colour, draw links between the sources to show ways in which they agree about the popularity of the Nazi regime. In another colour, draw links between the sources to show ways in which they disagree. Around the edge of the sources, write relevant own knowledge. Again, draw links to show the ways in which this agrees and disagrees with the sources.

Use Sources 1, 2 and 3 and your own knowledge.

To what extent do you agree with the view that the German people consented to Nazi rule because it pursued popular policies?

SOURCE 1

(From Detlev J K Peukert in Inside Nazi Germany: Conformity, Opposition, and Racism in Everyday Life, *published 1982)*

The recurrent legend, that Hitler rapidly succeeded in generating employment, is a reflection more of Nazi propaganda than of the reality of the Third Reich. Many people were impressed for a time in 1933 by the barrage of propaganda to the effect that the nation was now engaged in the decisive 'battle for work', but the elimination of unemployment in fact proceeded at a sluggish pace. The statistics were extensively manipulated. The sobering reality was becoming increasingly recognised by 1934, and matters remained thus until the inauguration of the big rearmament projects of 1936–7, which did indeed generate full employment, a critical juncture noted in many morale reports.

SOURCE 2

(From Ian Kershaw in The Hitler Myth, *published 1987)*

Although the extremes of the personality cult had probably gripped only a minority of the population, it was a minority with power and influence. Moreover, *elements* of the personality cult had attained far wider resonance and can be said to have affected the vast majority of the population. For most of the German population, Hitler stood for at least *some* things they admired, and for many Hitler had become the symbol and embodiment or the national revival which the Third Reich had in many respects been perceived to accomplish.

SOURCE 3

(From Richard J Evans in The Third Reich in Power, 1933–1939, *published 2005)*

Strength Through Joy was one of the most popular of the regime's innovations. So widespread was the use of Strength Through Joy's offerings that a popular joke maintained that the people were losing their strength through too much joy. Some despairing Social Democratic commentators concluded, therefore, that the programme did in the end have an important function in reconciling people, especially former opponents of the regime, to the Nazi government.

A consensus dictatorship?

Was the regime really popular?

Some historians have opposed the idea that the Nazi state was popular.

■ Some evidence from SOPADE, Gestapo and *Sicherheitsdienst* (the **SS**'s secret police, the **SD)** reports indicated dissatisfaction with living standards, the Nazi Party, and cynicism about government propaganda.

■ Martin Broszat disputes the argument that there was a lack of opposition to the regime and points to evidence of resistance from ordinary people, the elite and senior army generals. Some civil servants resisted Nazi initiative and generals tried to prevent complete Nazi control of the military.

■ Tim Mason argued that working-class discontent about declining living standards in the late 1930s pushed Hitler into war earlier than he had planned.

■ Karl Dietrich Bracher and Richard J Evans argue that the regime's terror apparatus made it impossible for people to express their dissatisfaction and therefore that the lack of opposition was not necessarily an indication of consent.

SOPADE, Gestapo and SD reports

Some of the evidence that historians use to examine public opinion in Nazi Germany comes from secret reports compiled by SOPADE, Gestapo and SD agents. These reports can give an interesting insight into public opinion, particularly as information was often collected secretly and not intended for public consumption.

Opposition and non-conformity

Through studying local archives, Broszat uncovered evidence of what he interpreted as widespread opposition to the Nazi state. Broszat found in his **Bavaria Project** of the 1970s and 1980s that civil disobedience and non-conformity to Nazi ideals were common. Broszat called this form of opposition *Resistenz*. For Broszat, any action which defied Nazi ideology, such as refusing to give the Nazi salute, listening to jazz, or buying goods from Jewish shops, constituted opposition because the Nazi regime attempted to establish total control over all aspects of life.

Others have questioned this idea and pointed out that discontent and non-conformity did not often translate into a desire to overthrow the Nazi state and that dissatisfaction was usually focused upon economic issues such as working hours. Walter Hofer also states that Broszat overstates the significance of *Resistenz* as he argues that it did not have any effect on Nazi policy.

Types of opposition

Detlev Peukert, whose research looked at the **Edelweiss Pirates** and the Swing Youth, conceptualised opposition as ranging from:

■ *active resistance,* such as attempts to overthrow the regime such as the Bomb Plot of 1944

■ *protest*, such as criticism of an aspect of Nazi policy. An example of this was Catholic priests reading out an **encyclical** from the Pope [*With Burning Concern, 1937*] condemning some Nazi ideas

■ *non-conformity*, that is, failing to adhere to Nazi ideals by, for example, listening to American jazz, dressing in an unconventional manner, telling anti-Nazi jokes or complaining about Nazi rule.

He argues that there was little active resistance, a little protest and significant levels of non-conformity in Nazi Germany.

Below are a sample Part (b) exam-style question and the three sources referred to in the question. Each source offers an interpretation of the issue raised by the question. Next to each source, summarise the interpretation offered by the source.

Use Sources 1, 2 and 3 and your own knowledge.

To what extent do you agree with the view that the Nazi regime enjoyed widespread popularity in the years 1933–1939?

SOURCE 1

(From Ian Kershaw in Resistance Without the People?, *published 1985)*

Working-class 'subcultures' did remain relatively impervious to the Nazis. Manifestations of discontent and signs of unrest became increasingly apparent from the mid-1930s onwards, *potentially* endangering the regime's stability and the accomplishment of its aims.

However, it would be as well not to make too much of this in terms of its effect on the functioning of the regime. Collective industrial 'protest' actions, through strikes, were small in scale and politically ineffective. Certainly, the regime's leadership did not give the impression that it was *politically* worried about the industrial working class.

SOURCE 2

(From Martyn Housden in Germans and their Opposition to the Third Reich, *published 1994)*

The most significant efforts at resistance came from the establishment sections of German society, that is to say the minor nobility, civil servants and, most notably, members of the officer corps.

Both workers and Christians refused to conform to Nazi demands in noteworthy ways. It appears, however, that worker unrest never really became unmanageable for the regime. The mixed strategies of propaganda, incentives, food on the table when it was most required, and Gestapo surveillance for the most part ensured the compliance of the working class in public. What opposition there was seems to have been most significant in private life, with groups of like-minded workers meeting secretly in order to keep alive their hopes for a better future.

SOURCE 3

(From Helmut Krausnick and Martin Broszat in Anatomy of the SS State, *published 1965)*

In the majority of cases, the political arrests made by the Gestapo in 1935–6 seem to have been for trifling offences. An interesting insight is provided by the reports of the Bavarian political police. Relatively the largest number of arrests seems to have been of persons denounced to the police for so-called subversive remarks. In 340 cases (almost 20 per cent) the reasons for the arrest are given as 'subversive remarks', 'insulting the Führer', 'defamation of the swastika', etc. The intention apparently was to use protective custody to nip in the bud any criticism of the National Socialist leadership. In the period 1935–6 this was an important function of the concentration camps.

The role of terror and repression

It could be argued that historians who focus on the idea of a 'consensus dictatorship' understate the scale of the terror.

The terror against the left

One reason for the lack of opposition to the Nazis was the scale of brutal repression directed against the left in 1933:

- The SA broke up SPD meetings and arrested, imprisoned and in some cases murdered members of the SPD and KPD. Armed SA members also took over trade union offices in May 1933.
- Concentration camps were established to detain the regime's opponents. In 1933, between 150,000 and 200,000 people were detained. Believing they had crushed the left, a third of prisoners were released in May 1933 and most of the remaining ones in August 1934.

The terror state

The Nazi state created many obstacles to resistance:

- Under the Nazis, people lost the right to freedom of speech and freedom of assembly. The Gestapo could arrest and hold people in custody for any reason or none at all, whilst a law of 24 April 1933 made seeking constitutional change a treasonable offence.
- From 1936, the head of the *Schutzstaffel* **(SS)**, Heinrich Himmler, was in charge of a huge network of terror and repression including the SS, SA, security service, the police and the Gestapo.
- The courts were used to suppress opposition in the mid-1930s. In 1935, 5,000 people were convicted of **high treason**; the prison population increased by 53,000 and 23,000 inmates of prisons were classed as political prisoners.
- The Gestapo may have been small in number, but it had a network of informants. The regime kept an eye on people via agents such as party officials and **Block Wardens** who monitored their local areas for signs of deviancy.
- The actions of the Gestapo and the SS made it extremely difficult for people to express discontent or opposition to the Nazis. Indeed, they were particularly active during the plebiscite campaigns, whose results cannot be accepted uncritically.
- *Gleichschaltung* meant that the Nazis were in control of most aspects of the state.

Terror and conformity

Between 1936 and 1939, the numbers held in concentration camps rose from 7500 to 21,000. The majority of inmates were classified as a-social: in Buchenwald 8892 of the 12,921 detainees were labelled as a-social. SS terror was used against these individuals to enforce conformity, rather than to counteract resistance to the Nazi state.

Was the Nazi state a consensus dictatorship?

It is hard to fully sustain the argument that the Nazi state was a consensus dictatorship given that political freedom was abolished, opponents of the regime smashed and an extensive terror network developed. There is also evidence that non-conformity and civil disobedience were widespread. Support for Hitler personally seems to have been strong, however, and many people credited the Nazis with certain successes. There was also widespread collaboration with the regime. Even so, support for the regime was never total and the Nazis failed in their mission to convert all those they deemed racially pure into enthusiastic Nazis.

Contrasting interpretations

Below are three sources offering interpretations regarding the extent to which the Nazi regime relied on terror and repression, rather than consent. Identify the interpretation offered in each source and complete the table below, indicating how far the sources agree with each other, and explaining your answer.

	Extent of agreement	Justification
Sources 1 and 2		
Sources 1 and 3		
Sources 2 and 3		

SOURCE 1

(From Robert Gellately in The Gestapo and German Society, *published 1990)*

There has been a tendency to suppose that the 'police state' relied on an extraordinarily large police force, which in turn could count on the collaboration of an army of paid agents and spies. . . . [however] there were certainly far too few to have accomplished their tasks even with the collaboration of other elements in the police network. . . . In all likelihood such 'spies' were not the police plants often supposed, but insiders – at the very least residents of long standing in the community who came forward more or less voluntarily . . . Gestapo power was built upon pre-existing beliefs, long-standing attitudes to crime, and the stigmas attached to those branded as criminals and delinquents. These prejudices worked in favour of whoever wore the police uniform, and against those whom they persecuted.

SOURCE 2

(From Claudia Coonz in The Nazi Conscience, *published 2003)*

A skilfully managed public relations campaign allowed moderate Germans to rationalise their support for Nazi rule. They could become 'yes but' Nazis – welcoming nationalism and economic recovery while dismissing Nazi crimes as incidental. The marketing strategy that allowed this kind of thinking was established by the end of 1934 and remained in place until the collapse of Nazi rule. No matter what the crime – whether the 'legal' theft of Jewish property, imprisonment in a concentration camp, or murder – it was committed in public. Hitler's benign public image and careful news management minimised their impact. Media reporting on concentration camps and mass arrests described Nazi terror as protective, and protesting voices were discredited as foreign influenced.

SOURCE 3

(From Roger Griffin in The Nature of Fascism, *published 1991)*

The Concordat was just one component in the complex strategy the Nazi leadership had to adopt in order to neutralize opposition. The Church succeeded in resisting Nazi attempts to found a 'National Church.' Nonetheless, illiberal nationalism and anti-Communism had been rife among both Protestant and Catholic clergy ensuring collusion or passivity in the crucial years of Nazi rule. In contrast, another potential source of dissent, the schools and universities, were Nazified with extraordinary rapidity, a process vastly facilitated by the deep inroads volkish nationalism had already made into the academic world before 1933. Curricular, textbooks, student assignments and lectures were soon applying Aryan principles to every discipline from music to physics. The press was brought into line by buy-outs, censorship, thinly veiled coercion and the Nazification of personnel.

An efficient state?

There has also been much historical debate over the structure of the Nazi state and the extent of Hitler's power.

Strong dictator?

Immediately after the Second World War, the image of the Nazi state was efficient and hierarchically organised, with all power concentrated in Hitler's hands. At the **Nuremberg Trials** in 1945, senior Nazis supported this view by defending themselves on the grounds that they were just following Hitler's orders.

Intentionalist historians viewed the Nazi state as **totalitarian** and organised to carry out Hitler's will, which was the basis for law after the Enabling Act was passed. Hitler's *intentions* were therefore considered very important in explaining state policy.

Weak dictator?

Since the 1960s this interpretation of Hitler's power and the workings of the Nazi state has been challenged by historical evidence that organisation and decision-making processes were chaotic and inefficient.

People's impressions of Hitler are often of an all-powerful leader with total control. However, in perceiving him in this way, we may be falling for the 'Hitler Myth'. He was frequently lazy, and often out of Berlin in his holiday home on **Obersalzberg**, where he gave few direct orders, preferring to relax, watch films and sleep in. Was Hitler in actual fact a weak dictator, who did not control decision-making in Nazi Germany?

A chaotic and polycratic state

Hitler's weakness seemed to be supported by research revealing that the Nazi state was very chaotic:

- There were no clear decision-making procedures, and often no clear lines of accountability.
- Structures were often duplicated and overlapping in their functions, creating inefficiency. From 1936, for example, both the Office of the Four Year Plan and the Economics Ministry had authority over economic policy.
- Parts of the Nazi state were able to build up vast power and often competed with one another for dominance. Nazi Party bureaucracy sometimes competed with state institutions like government ministries and the independent **Gauleiter** who were only accountable to Hitler.

This picture of a chaotic and disorganised state with many different powerbases has been characterised as **polycracy**. The idea that Hitler was in fact a weak dictator is supported by **structuralist** historians such as Broszat and Hans Mommsen who investigated the operation of the Nazi state and argued that the state was too chaotic for Hitler to have been in full command of it.

Chaos and decision-making

When decision-making in Nazi Germany is analysed, it often appears that others and not Hitler initiated action:

- In 1935 the **Nuremberg Laws** were introduced following pressure from local Nazi Party organisations for stronger action against Jews. At the Nuremberg Rally of 1935, Hitler announced the Laws: he had originally planned to discuss foreign policy in this speech.
- **Kristallnacht** in November 1938 was orchestrated by Goebbels and much of the action occurred spontaneously at local level. Hitler had authorised the action, however.
- Nazi official Philipp Bouhler brought Hitler's attention to a letter from the father of a disabled child asking Hitler to allow his son to be killed. Hitler authorised this and a programme to kill mentally and physically disabled children. This policy was known as **Aktion T4**.

Below are a sample Part (b) exam-style question and the three sources referred to in the question. In one colour, draw links between the sources to show ways in which they agree about the structure and efficiency of the Nazi state. In another colour, draw links between the sources to show ways in which they disagree. Around the edge of the sources, write relevant own knowledge. Again, draw links to show the ways in which this agrees and disagrees with the sources.

Use Sources 1, 2 and 3 and your own knowledge.

To what extent do you agree with the view that Hitler exercised 'absolute dictatorial power' between 1933 and 1939?

SOURCE 1

(From Ernst Fraenkel in The Dual State, *published 1942)*

Absolute dictatorial power is exercised by the Leader and Chancellor either personally or through his subordinate authorities. His sole decision determines how power shall be wielded. His powers were derived from the new German 'constitution': the law passed by the government on July 2nd 1934*. With few exceptions the Leader and Chancellor exercises absolute dictatorial powers, no legal limitation to his power exists.

*On July 2nd 1934 Hitler was granted the powers of the President in addition to his existing powers as Chancellor.

SOURCE 2

(From Martin Broszat in The Hitler State, *published 1981)*

The more the organisational jungle of the National Socialist regime spread out the less chance there was of restoring any rationally organized and consistent policy making. The proliferation of institutions and special powers, which caused an increasingly bitter struggle within government, contributed to a radicalisation of policy, which took place amidst a progressive division of power, an increasingly fragmented process where any overall co-ordination and regulation was missing.

Admittedly Hitler's obsessive preoccupation with specific ideological and political aims proved to be a decisive driving force behind Nazi policy. But the Führer was not in the least able to decide on the specifics of policy.

SOURCE 3

(From Ian Kershaw in The Hitler Myth, *published 1987)*

The popular notion of a Führer standing over and above the wrangles of everyday politics was not wholly mythical. From 1935–6 onwards, Hitler did in reality withdraw increasingly from involvement in the day-to-day running of government. He left the ordinary business of government more and more to the overlapping and competing ministries, and special organisations like that of the 'Four Year Plan', which turned internal government in Germany into administrative chaos, while he concentrated in growing measure on matters of diplomatic and foreign policy.

Challenge the historian

Source 1 above provides an interpretation of the nature of Hitler's leadership. Read the source, identify the interpretation offered by the source, and use your own knowledge to provide a counter-argument, challenging the interpretation offered by the source.

Interpretation offered by the source

_____

_____

Counter-argument

_____

_____

_____

_____

An efficient state?

Despite the chaotic nature of the Nazi state and the absence of direct orders from Hitler, Nazi policy generally seems to have developed to reflect Hitler's ideas. In racial policy, for example, Hitler's anti-Semitism was reflected in the persecution of Jews. Ian Kershaw sought to reconcile the chaos of the Nazi state with the apparent influence of Hitler's ideas.

The role of Hitler

All decisions were supposed to emanate from Hitler, and in some areas Hitler did directly control decision-making. Where Hitler was particularly interested in policy, he took a dominant role. Hitler steered foreign policy by first rejecting the **Treaty of Versailles** and then developing expansionist plans:

- In 1936, Hitler took the decision to remilitarise the Rhineland against the advice of his generals, and he was instrumental in the *Anschluss* in 1938.

- It was Hitler's decision to push forward with an expansionist policy in Eastern Europe in the late 1930s, as can be seen in his 1936 Four Year Plan memorandum, urging the creation of a ***Wehrwirtschaft*** (war economy) to enable a large-scale war to be fought within four years, and in his war plans, known as Operation Green.

- Hitler's power in this area can be seen in the removal of two senior military figures, Fritsch and Blomberg, who had expressed reservations about the plan for war that Hitler presented at the so-called **Hossbach meeting** in 1937.

Working towards the Führer

In other areas, while Hitler did not always make direct decisions, policy was developed which reflected his wishes. Kershaw's explanation for this is that many people within the Nazi state took decisions by 'working towards the Führer': that is, people sought to anticipate what Hitler would want and formulated policy on this basis. By this process policy developed, in the words of one Nazi bureaucrat, 'along the lines that the Führer would wish'.

In the chaos of the Nazi state, 'working towards the Führer' may also have been not just a way to be guided in what decisions to make but also a method of potential career advancement: those who could best implement Hitler's will were most likely to win favour and power. Through the mechanism of 'working towards the Führer', Hitler's vision provided the overall inspiration for policy.

Examples of 'working towards the Führer'

- Goering was prepared to enact Hitler's aim of a *Wehrwirtschaft*. He was given far-reaching powers by Hitler over economic policy as **Plenipotentiary** of the Office of the Four Year Plan in 1936. In contrast, Hjalmar Schacht, the Economics Minister, was sidelined after this time as he did not want to devote the level of resources to rearmament that Hitler wanted. He was ultimately replaced by Walther Funk.

- Goebbels orchestrated Kristallnacht partly because he was out of favour with Hitler following an affair with a Czech actress (Czechs were considered racially inferior by Hitler). Kristallnacht was Goebbels' attempt to win favour with Hitler by 'working towards' him.

- In pursuing the idea of murdering disabled children, Bouhler was 'working towards the Führer': Hitler sought to create a racially 'pure' society in which people who were not fully fit and strong were eradicated from the 'race'.

RAG – Rate the sources

Below are a sample Part (b) exam-style question and the sources referred to in the question. Read the question, study the sources and, using three coloured pens, underline them in Red, Amber and Green to show:

Red: Counter-arguments and counter-evidence provided by the source
Amber: Evidence that supports this interpretation
Green: The interpretation offered by the question

Use Sources 1, 2 and 3 and your own knowledge.

How far do you agree that the Nazi government was too chaotic to allow Hitler to be a strong leader?

SOURCE 1

(From Richard J Evans in The Third Reich in Power, 1933–1939, *published 2005)*

Hitler's working habits were irregular. His Bohemianism was evident in his lifestyle: he often stayed up well into the small hours watching movies in his private cinema, and he was often very late to rise the next day. Hitler's Bohemian lifestyle did not mean, however, that he was lazy or inactive, or that he withdrew from domestic politics after 1933. When the occasion demanded, he could intervene powerfully and decisively. Hitler, in other words, was erratic rather than lazy in his working habits. In areas where he did take a real interest, he did not hesitate to give a direct lead even in matters of detail.

SOURCE 2

(From Ian Kershaw in Hitler 1889–1936: Hubris, *published 1998)*

Hitler's personalised form of rule invited radical initiatives from below and offered such initiatives backing, so long as they were in line with his broadly defined goals. This promoted ferocious competition at all levels of the regime, among competing agencies, and among individuals within those agencies. In the Darwinist jungle of the Third Reich, the way to power and advancement was through anticipating the 'Führer will', and, without waiting for directives, taking initiatives to promote what were presumed to be Hitler's aims and wishes. Through 'working towards the Führer', initiatives were taken, pressures created, legislation instigated – all in ways which fell into line with what were taken to be Hitler's aims, and without the dictator necessarily having to dictate. The result was continuing radicalisation of policy in a direction which brought Hitler's own ideological imperatives more plainly into view as practicable policy options.

SOURCE 3

(From David Welch in Hitler: Profile of a Dictator, *published 2001)*

The first point to note is that despite the image of a strong leader, Hitler had always found it difficult to make up his mind in times of crisis. In June 1934 Hitler agreed to the purge of the SA ('Night of the Long Knives') only belatedly and reluctantly, he shelved dealing with the economic crisis of 1935–1936 when a serious shortage of foodstuffs arose, and in September 1938 Hitler almost lost his nerve in the Sudetenland crisis. Hitler's style of leadership had led to a chaotic form of administrative anarchy. It is not surprising to discover, therefore, that his foreign policy, governed as it was by a combination of ideology, opportunism and instinct, should be equally inconsistent and contradictory.

An efficient state?

The nature of the Nazi state

Examining the operation of the Nazi state reveals insights into the nature of Hitler's power and the workings of the government.

Reasons for 'working towards the Führer'

Simply acknowledging that many officials were 'working towards the *Führer*' does not explain their motives. One of the reasons why German officials worked towards the Führer was ideological: according to the *Führerprinzip*, all power and authority rested with Hitler. People may also have sought to please the Führer to advance their careers. Another reason, according to Ian Kershaw, is that the Hitler Myth had such power that people actually believed in the idea of Hitler as a messianic figure who would save Germany and therefore they wished to work to enact his vision.

The Third Reich: a Darwinian Jungle?

A government in which officials were 'working towards the Führer' gave Hitler a strange sort of power: he was the dictator who did not need to dictate. However, there is controversy over the extent to which Hitler deliberately established the system of chaotic rule. It may have been that the chaos was a product of Hitler's Social Darwinist view that the strongest person or idea will and should prevail. Thus Hitler may have felt that a chaotic and competitive system was best.

Cumulative radicalisation

The nature of Nazi government may also explain why the Nazi state became more and more extreme after the mid-1930s. One explanation for this is that an absence of legal restraints, the mechanism of 'working towards the Führer' and a context in which human life was not valuable combined to create ever more radical policy. This process was referred to by Mommsen as **cumulative radicalisation.** Through this process, the Nazi state became increasingly dominated by the SS police system and racial and foreign policy became ever more extreme. This idea will be further explored in the next section in connection with the origins of the Holocaust.

An efficient state with an all-powerful ruler?

Hitler was not in control of all decision-making in Nazi Germany. The Nazi state had a chaotic and **polycratic** structure, as can be seen in the organisation of economic policy. Decision-making processes were not clear and Hitler did not control all aspects of policy. Nevertheless, Hitler intervened directly in the areas that he thought were the most important such as foreign policy. Furthermore, Hitler's vision provided inspiration for Nazi policy through the mechanism of 'working towards the Führer'. Others depended upon Hitler's favour to advance in their careers and gain power.

The following sources relate to the structure and efficiency of the Nazi state. Read the guidance detailing what you need to know about this controversy. Having done this, write a Part (b) exam-style question using the sources.

SOURCE 1

(From Geoffrey P Megargee in War of Annihilation, *published 2007)*

A careful examination of the *Führerprinzip* reveals a system that was not really so rigid as it appeared on the surface. It depended not so much on a vision that the leader imposed on his subordinates, but more on a common set of goals and assumptions that they all shared. In political terms, as Hitler put it, "The Führer is the Party and the Party is the Führer." Or, on another occasion: "The leader must give orders that express the common feelings of his men." The *Führerprinzip* did not eliminate initiative, but rather emphasised a common purpose and shared responsibility. All of this adds up to a command system that provided for both obedience and initiative in pursuit of a common aim, with a high degree of teamwork.

SOURCE 2

(From Hans Mommsen in Cumulative Radicalisation, *published 1997)*

The assumption that the fragmentation of politics arose from a deliberate divide-and-rule strategy on Hitler's part is misleading. Rather, this was a reflection of the social-darwinist conviction that the best man would ultimately prevail. This technique meant in the long run that a great deal of energy was spent on feuds between different agencies. These mechanisms of government were, however, of the utmost importance for the internal development of the regime. This social-darwinist struggle led to an escalating ruthlessness in pursuit of the extreme goals of the Nazi movement, and thus to a process of cumulative radicalisation. Individual chieftains felt compelled to fight competitors with all means at their disposal. Each office-holder tried to gain the special sympathies of the Führer by appearing as a fanatical fighter for the realisation of Hitler's goals.

SOURCE 3

(From Eberhard Jackel in Hitler in History, *published 1989)*

It is not altogether false to call Hitler a weak dictator. As late as 1938 he had not been strong enough to change ministers at will, and he had also not been strong enough to wage war at will. But much of his strength lay precisely in his weakness. It enabled him to conceal his ultimate goals and disclose them only gradually. It also enabled him to order certain acts without being identified with them. When the mentally ill were killed by the tens of thousands, the practice met with widespread opposition, but Hitler was generally not identified with it. A letter written by one leading Nazi woman to another is evidence of this, "people are still clinging to the hope that the Führer knows nothing about these things, that he cannot possibly know, otherwise he would stop them."

Use Sources 1, 2 and 3 and your own knowledge.

How far do you agree that _____

_____

Explain your answer, using Sources 1, 2 and 3 and your own knowledge of the issues related to this controversy.

Recommended reading

Below is a list of suggested further reading on this topic.

- *The Nazi Dictatorship*, pages 69–92, Ian Kershaw (2000)
- *Hitler: Profile of a Dictator,* David Welch (2001)
- *Germans Against Nazism: Nonconformity, Opposition and Resistance in the Third Reich*, pages 15–36, Francis R Nicosia and Lawrence D Stokes (1990)

Exam focus

On pages 87–89 is a sample answer to the Part (b) exam-style question on this page. Read the answer and the examiner comments around it.

(b) Use Sources 1, 2 and 3 and your own knowledge.

To what extent do you agree with the view that German society under the Nazis was characterised by 'collective compliance'?

Explain your answer, using Sources 1, 2 and 3 and your own knowledge of the issues related to this controversy. (40 marks)

SOURCE 1

(From Ian Kershaw in The Hitler Myth, *published 1987)*

In contrast to the Nazi Party, the Führer was associated with the spectacular foreign policy successes and the celebration of national triumphs, representing the 'sunny side' of the regime. And for the maintenance of the 'Führer myth' it was vital that success continued, that the external 'national' policy of the regime remained sunny, as it effectively did for a number of years following the first major triumphs in 1935–6.

Although the overwhelming majority of the population clearly wanted 'national success' – the restoration of Germany's power and glory in Europe – it was just as clearly unwilling to entertain the idea of major sacrifices to attain them. This amounted to a sort of 'working basis' of the 'Führer myth', which Hitler recognized and complied with by providing a series of rapid foreign policy and diplomatic coups.

SOURCE 2

(From Tim Mason in Social Policy in the Third Reich, *published 1993)*

Every time the state tampered with the rights or living standards of the working class, it provoked a wave of resentment, which really represented a kind of passive opposition. Whether it was the attempt to limit wages in 1938–9 or the massive, concerted assault by the government along the entire front of social policy in 1939, the occasions and causes of discontent were clear and specific. Absenteeism, loafing on the job, carelessness, taking sick leave and insubordination assumed the character of a collective protest in this context. In many individual instances as well, workers would react in a hostile fashion when they were denied permission to change jobs or else they would try to provoke their dismissal in order to accept a better position.

SOURCE 3

(From Hugh Trevor-Roper in Germans against Hitler, *published 1964)*

The Blood-Bath of June 30, 1934, set the tone for Hitler's rule. It showed that it was not only a dictatorship, but a criminal dictatorship. It also showed that German society at all levels accepted such a dictatorship. For ten years of repression, aggression, violence and murder no visible conspiracy or revolt threatened it.

Attempts have been made to represent certain sections of the German population as anti-Nazi. These attempts are vain. The Catholic Church has its individual heroes, but as an institution its record is of eager compliance. The Socialists resisted with their votes, but accepted their ultimate fate. All this collective compliance can be explained. To every class of Germans Hitler offered something: employment, land, status, self-assurance, revenge.

German society under the Nazis was characterised by 'collective compliance' to a large extent. 'Collective compliance' was achieved through popular foreign policy, the 'Führer myth', programmes such as Strength Through Joy, propaganda and Terror.

Clearly, there is a great deal of evidence in the sources that German society under the Nazis was characterised by 'collective compliance' (Source 3). Source 3, for example, argues that in general terms, the Catholic Church, and even members of the Social Democrats, 'accepted their ultimate fate'. He argues that the collective compliance was explained by the fact that Hitler was able to offer something to everyone. Hitler's popularity is also a key feature of the interpretation offered by Source 1. Here, Kershaw argues that Hitler's foreign policy was widely admired. Specifically, he argues that the regime had a 'sunny side'. Kershaw is referring to foreign policy successes, such as the Saar plebiscite of 1935, the remilitarisation of the Rhineland in 1936, and the Anschluss of 1938. Each one of these expanded German territory, and the first two represented the regaining of territory lost under the Treaty of Versailles. In this sense, Kershaw is right to characterise them as 'national success — the restoration of Germany's power and glory in Europe'. It is no wonder that the plebiscites of 1935, 1936 and 1938 showed such high levels of support for Hitler's foreign policy. For example, in the latter two plebiscites, 99 percent of voters approved of Hitler's foreign policy and even in the 1935 plebiscite Hitler won 90 percent of the popular vote. Evidently, Source 3 is broadly correct to argue that German society was characterised by 'collective compliance' because Hitler's foreign policy appealed to the vast majority of Germans who therefore, to some extent, were prepared to back the regime.

Evidence of 'collective compliance' goes far beyond the support that Hitler gained through foreign policy. Source 1 argues that the 'Führer myth' underpinned the stability of the regime by portraying Hitler as the saviour of Germany, a modern-day Jesus or Teutonic Knight, who was the representative of the nation, and in this sense above politics. The 'Führer myth' was created by Goebbels, the Nazi propaganda chief, who was appointed Minister of Popular Enlightenment and Propaganda in 1933. He was able to cultivate the 'Führer myth' by careful control of the German media. The 'Führer myth' was spread in newsreels and by radio. Newspaper editors were put under enormous pressure not to criticise the regime and Hitler was associated with national successes such as the 1936 Olympics, which created a national 'feel-good factor'. Source 2 mentions resentment in the working class, particularly following the 'attempt to limit wages in 1938–9'. The regime was aware of this and tried to counter it through programmes such as 'Strength Through Joy' which offered luxuries, such as holidays, to the working class. For example, in 1934, a poll of 32,000 workers for Siemens, based in Berlin, revealed that 28,500 had taken advantage of holidays provided by 'Strength

The introduction is weak because it does not mention any of the sources and it does not link the quote used in the question to the correct source. Part (b) essays are expected to focus on the interpretation of the sources and therefore the omission of the sources from the introduction suggests a lack of focus.

This paragraph clearly links aspects of two of the sources. It cross-references the interpretation of Source 3 with the interpretation of Source 1, showing how these interpretations complement each other.

Here, the candidate shows detailed and focused own knowledge, and links this own knowledge to the sources and to the question.

through Joy'. Indeed, SOPADE reports indicated that 'Strength Through Joy' was genuinely popular with the German working class. Finally, Source 3 points to the fact that 'To every class of Germans Hitler offered something' such as employment to the unemployed in 1933–1934. In this way, German society was characterised by 'collective compliance' to a large extent because propaganda persuaded people to trust Hitler and the regime had a 'sunny side' that went beyond foreign policy and included events such as the Olympics, and programmes such as 'Strength Through Joy'.

Here, the candidate brings in a further interpretation from their own knowledge, linking it to the interpretation offered by Source 2. This places the sources within the wider debate of this controversy, showing detailed knowledge of the issues linked to the controversy.

While the sources indicate that there was evidence of 'collective compliance', Source 2 argues that there was widespread resentment among the working class. In spite of the success of 'Strength Through Joy', Source 2 argues that the working class refused to accept the government's attempts to deny workers rights or reduce their living standards. He argues that 'Absenteeism, loafing on the job, carelessness, taking sick leave and insubordination' were signs of 'collective protest' in the context of government policy which was designed to deny workers rights. Further evidence of discontent comes from Broszat's Bavaria Project which documented widespread acts of civil disobedience and non-conformity. Broszat, like Mason in Source 2, argues that the context in which these acts occurred indicate that they were politically significant. Specifically, Broszat argues that any act of 'Resistenz' against a government attempting control over all aspects of life amounts to political dissent. Indeed, Mason's description of hostile reactions from workers seeking dismissal can be read as a political statement as it was a response to government policy. Even Source 1 implies that domestic policy was problematic for the Nazis. It is significant that 'the first major triumphs' took place in 1935–1936, during the peak of workers' unrest. In this sense, Hitler's foreign policy triumphs were an attempt to win over the German working class who had become disillusioned because of high food prices. Significantly, Hitler's successes do seem to have won over the working class as the resistance of 1938–1939, mentioned in Source 2, was less notable in terms of numbers on strike than the first wave of strikes in 1935. Therefore, while there was widespread 'Resistenz', Mason, in Source 2, overstates the significance of 'passive opposition' because the fact that the Nazis could regain support from the working class with foreign policy successes indicates that working class insubordination was aimed more at improving their own situation than undermining the regime. In this sense, the argument of Source 2 does not contradict Source 3's claim that there was widespread 'collective compliance'.

At the end of this paragraph, the candidate considers the relationship between the interpretations of Sources 2 and 3. Significantly, the candidate is weighing the interpretations, showing that they understand that the different interpretations, while different, are not contradictory.

Nevertheless, it is worth considering the impact of Terror, mentioned in Source 3, on German society. While Source 1 indicates that Hitler was genuinely popular, Source 3 argues that 'the Blood-Bath of June 30, 1934, set the tone for Hitler's rule'. Source 3 thus suggests that German society was characterised more by collective fear than by 'collective compliance'. Indeed, the Nazis constructed an extensive 'Terror State' and, in 1933, between 150,000 and 200,000 were held in 'protective custody' in concentration camps. Equally, every group of houses had a Gestapo Block Warden who monitored the local area for signs of deviancy in order to nip in the bud any signs of political resistance. However, Source 3 presents a different interpretation of the significance of Terror. The 'Blood-Bath' mentioned in the first sentence is a reference to the Night of the Long Knives. Significantly, the massacre of the SA leadership was welcomed by the majority of Germans and therefore, rather than inducing widespread fear, this example of Nazi Terror won widespread approval. This is one of the reasons why so many Germans (90 percent) voted for Hitler to take the powers of the presidency in the 1934 plebiscite. Terror in 1933 against the left wing was also presented as defensive. Although the use of Terror appears to undermine the claim that German society was characterised by 'collective compliance', in reality Terror consolidated this compliance in two ways. First, it stopped any organised resistance, but more significantly it allowed Goebbels to present Hitler as the defender of the nation, an important part of the 'Führer myth' described in Source 1.

In conclusion, Source 3 is correct to argue that German society under the Nazis was characterised by 'collective compliance' because Source 1 and Source 3 agree, and the argument of Source 2 does not explicitly contradict this.

Here, the candidate clearly understands the significance of the date mentioned in the source, stating that June 30, 1934 was the Night of the Long Knives. This is evidence of detailed own knowledge and careful reading of the source.

The conclusion, like the introduction, is weak. It provides a basic summary of the interpretations of the sources, but does not reach and substantiate an overall judgement.

32/40

This essay is an analytical response integrating own knowledge with the interpretations of the sources. Outside the introduction and conclusion, it develops a sophisticated argument, raising points that clearly support the interpretation in the question, and showing how points that appear contradictory actually uphold the picture of a generally compliant German society. A better introduction and conclusion would have made the argument explicit and therefore allowed the examiner to award a mark in Level 5.

Moving from Level 4 to Level 5

The Exam Focus at the end of Section 2 provided a Level 5 essay. The essay here achieves a Level 4 as the introduction and conclusion are weak. Make a list of the key features of the introduction and conclusion provided in the Section 2 Exam Focus. Rewrite the introduction and conclusion of this essay, ensuring that it reflects the features needed for Level 5.

Section 6: Life in wartime Germany, 1939–1945

An overview of the Second World War

On 1 September 1939, Nazi Germany invaded Poland. On 3 September, Britain and France declared war on Germany and the Second World War began.

The causes of the Second World War

Hitler's aggressive foreign policy

As part of Hitler's plan for *Lebensraum*, Germany had already expanded its military and annexed Austria and Czechoslovakia. Britain and France felt that they could not allow Germany to become excessively dominant and acted when Germany invaded Poland in 1939.

A weak international system

Hitler had the opportunity to ignore the **Treaty of Versailles** and launch aggressive actions because the international system was weak in the 1930s.

- The USA and **USSR** were **isolationist**.
- Britain and France were not in a strong position to uphold international order as they both had problems resulting from the Depression.
- Keen to avoid war and feeling that the Treaty of Versailles was excessively harsh, Britain followed a policy of **appeasement** which may have actually encouraged Hitler to be more aggressive.
- Concerted action by the USSR, France and Britain might have prevented Hitler's attack on Poland but the three countries could not work together: eventually the USSR signed the **Nazi–Soviet Pact**, which allowed Poland to be carved up between themselves and the Germans. Hitler could now attack Poland without fear of **Soviet** opposition.

The course of the war

1939–1941 – German successes

After the Nazis had overrun Poland in four weeks, using the technique of **blitzkrieg**, a period of **phoney war** began. This was broken by the invasion of Scandinavia in March 1940 where the British navy unsuccessfully engaged the Germans near the coast of Norway. Subsequently, Germany conquered the **Low Countries** in quick succession before defeating the British and French armies to take control of France by June 1940.

After failing to push Britain out of the war during the **Battle of Britain** in summer 1940, Hitler launched an invasion of the **Soviet Union** in June 1941. Initially, this attack met with considerable success as the *Wehrmacht* rapidly seized large amounts of territory. Meanwhile, German forces engaged the **Allies** in North Africa.

Late 1941–1943 – The tide turns

With the USA now in the war following the Japanese attack on **Pearl Harbor** in December 1941, the Germans started to struggle. In North Africa, British forces defeated the German army at El Alamein in November 1942 while, in the Soviet Union, the Germans were overstretched and suffered a serious defeat at Stalingrad where the entire Sixth Army of 300,000 ultimately surrendered in January 1943. From this point onwards the **Red Army** started to defeat the *Wehrmacht*, while from May 1943 the Allies started to win the **Battle of the Atlantic**.

1944–1945 – defeat

US, British and Canadian forces opened up a third **front** in northern France (a second front existing by now in Italy) on **D-Day**, 6 June 1944, and pushed the Germans back from the west while, at the same time, the Soviet Union had a string of successes against the Germans in **Operation Bagration**. It was now only a matter of time until the total defeat of Germany and of the Nazis. On 30 April 1945, Hitler committed suicide when Soviet soldiers reached Berlin. The European war was effectively over.

The course of the Second World War

Below is the axis of a graph. Using the information on the opposite page, plot key events from the Second World War onto the axis. First, plot each event in the appropriate place on the horizontal axis (that is to say, place it next to the appropriate date). Secondly, reach a judgement about the success of the German war effort at this point, and plot the event at the appropriate point on the vertical axis. Once you have plotted all key events, join up the dots to create a graph representing Germany's successes and failures in the Second World War. This will form a useful reference tool as you work through this section.

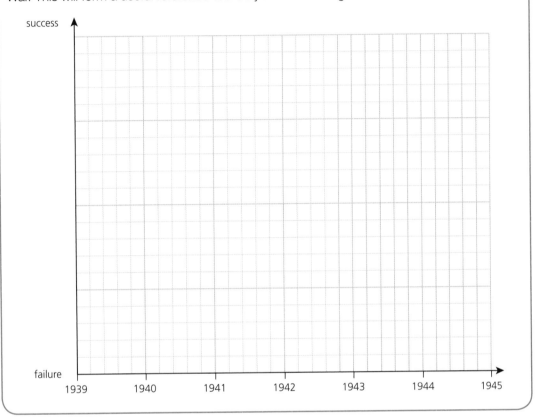

 Recommended reading

Below is a list of suggested further reading on this section.

- *Hitler, 1936–45: Nemesis*, pages 751–94, Ian Kershaw (2000)
- *The German Dictatorship,* pages 495–568, Karl Dietrich Bracher (1991)
- *Hitler: A Study in Tyranny (Abridged Edition)*, pages 321–484, Alan Bullock (1971)

Civilian morale during the war

Despite evidence that many Germans were not in favour of going to war in 1939, early successes helped to bolster morale and support for the regime. However, support declined and more opposition began to emerge, particularly after Stalingrad.

Morale

While conditions in wartime Germany were not easy, Hitler made it a priority to try to maintain supplies on the home front. Indeed, it was not until near the end of the war that the German people suffered from the extreme shortages experienced during the First World War.

A number of measures helped to maintain support for the regime early on in the war:

- While meat was rationed, it remained at the reasonable level of 500g until April 1942.
- Extra rations were given at Christmas and for those in strenuous jobs.
- Until 1944, rations were in excess of the minimum calories required.
- Early victories in Poland, Norway, Denmark, Luxembourg, Belgium and France helped maintain morale.
- Propaganda also may have had an impact.
- Hitler resisted Albert Speer's calls later in the war to **mobilise** women. Hitler felt that maintaining traditional roles for women would be better for morale.

Declining support

After 1942, evidence is that people were now sometimes critical of Hitler and that non-conformity and cynicism were rife. A number of factors caused morale and support for the regime to weaken:

- Working conditions were difficult: hours at work increased, particularly in armaments factories.
- Some young people reacted negatively to the militarisation of the Hitler Youth after 1939.
- Defeat at Stalingrad could not be covered up by the regime as the scale of the losses was so great. The high rate of casualties on the **Eastern Front** damaged morale and provoked some criticism of Hitler who was by this point rarely seen in public: Goebbels was much more the public face of the regime from 1943.
- Allied bombing of German cities seems to have reduced morale in some areas, such as in the Rhineland. Allied bombing killed 305,000 people, injured 780,000 and destroyed 2 million homes in Germany. Bombing raids caused firestorms which killed tens of thousands in Hamburg in 1943 and Dresden in 1945.
- The Soviet advance from 1943 and the consequent threat of Soviet invasion caused fear among the German public.
- The **V1 and V2** in a 1944 rocket campaign against south-eastern England and Allied ports like Antwerp failed to have a decisive impact on the course of the war and caused morale to decline.

Why was civilian morale maintained?

While support for Hitler and the regime may have reduced during the war, morale did not collapse entirely, unlike at the end of the First World War. The Nazi regime was removed by foreign powers and not by opposition from within Germany: active opposition still only involved a small number of people.

Goebbels continued his efforts to promote support for the regime and attempted to respond to weakening morale by urging perseverance. He famously called upon a crowd to support 'total war' in a speech at the **Sportpalast** in Berlin in February 1943. Films such as *The Adventures of Baron Munchausen* (1943) and *Kolberg* (1945) tried to encourage patriotic feeling.

Spot the mistake

Below are a sample Part (a) exam-style question and a paragraph written in answer to this question. Why does this paragraph not get into Level 4? Once you have identified the mistake, rewrite the paragraph so that it displays the qualities of Level 4. The mark scheme on page 117 will help you.

'The Nazi regime faced no serious opposition during the Second World War.' How far do you agree with this opinion?

> Many historians have questioned the level of support for the Nazi regime. Robert Gellately argues that the Nazi regime was a 'consensus dictatorship'. His book, The Gestapo and German Society, published in 1991, presents a study of the city Würzburg, in which he argues that the Gestapo was not the all-powerful terror network that is often imagined. Gellately argues that there were only 21 Gestapo officers for the whole of the Würzburg area. Rather than keeping everyone under surveillance, the Gestapo in Würzburg relied heavily on information from ordinary people to root out those who did not conform to the ideals of the Nazi regime. This is supported by evidence from SOPADE files and it should be remembered that the Nazi regime was very popular after Hitler remilitarised the Rhineland and after Germany united with Austria. In this way, it is correct to argue that the Nazi regime faced no serious opposition because the Nazi regime was essentially a 'consensus dictatorship'.

Complete the paragraph

Below are a sample Part (a) exam-style question and a paragraph written in answer to this question. The paragraph contains a point and a concluding explanatory link back to the question, but lacks examples. Complete the paragraph, adding examples in the space provided.

'The morale of the German public remained remarkably high during the Second World War.' How far do you agree with this view?

> From 1942 to 1944, German morale did remain remarkably high.
>
> _____
>
> _____
>
> _____
>
> _____
>
> In this way, German morale remained remarkably high because of Nazi efforts to sustain fighting spirit in the difficult days of 1942–1944.

Opposition during the war

Christian opposition

■ The Catholic Church continued to speak out where they felt their interests or values were threatened. In 1941, a couple of incidents illustrate this: large protests against an order to remove crucifixes from Bavarian schools caused the order to be reversed and Bishop Galen attacked the **Aktion T4** 'euthanasia' programme, whose existence was subsequently covered up.

■ Individual Protestant churchmen attacked the regime. Dietrich Bonhoeffer spoke out against the regime and was arrested in 1943 and executed in 1945.

Youthful opposition

■ Some **Edelweiss Pirates** became more active during the war, working with the **left-wing underground** and helping to smuggle out escaped prisoners of war. The leaders of the Pirates in Cologne were publicly hanged for their activities in 1944.

■ The White Rose student movement was formed in Munich in 1942. The movement urged Germans to reject Nazi values on ethical grounds. The group distributed anti-Nazi letters and leaflets. Brother and sister Hans and Sophie Scholl were beheaded for their activities in the movement in 1943.

Left-wing opposition

■ Robert Uhrig established **resistance cells** in factories: in the summer of 1941, there were 89 of these in Berlin.

■ There were also communist groups in Hamburg and Mannheim and various active socialist groups, such as Red Patrol.

■ Communist network **Rote Kappelle**, some of whose members had access to sensitive information, collected intelligence and engaged in the distribution of anti-Nazi leaflets. The network was uncovered and destroyed by the military intelligence in 1942. Other Communist groups led by Wilhelm Knöchel were broken up in 1943.

■ There was some active underground resistance on the left but these isolated groups did not have a great impact on undermining the regime.

Conservative opposition

A number of conservative opposition groups sought a restoration of the rule of law and an end to the war:

■ A group around Carl Goerdeler included officials and diplomats, such as Ulrich von Hassell.

■ The Kreisau Circle was a conservative group led by **Junker** Helmuth Graf von Moltke which by the end of the war had contacts with the **left-wing** opposition and opponents of the regime in the army.

■ In the army some officers rejected the regime after Stalingrad and sought to overthrow it. In the 1944 Bomb Plot, an army group sought to assassinate Hitler and seize power. Assassin Stauffenberg's bomb did not kill Hitler, however, and the plot was uncovered. As a result, 22 generals were executed and Field Marshal Rommel was prevailed upon to commit suicide.

Why did opposition not succeed in overthrowing the regime?

■ Lack of support: even though the German people were less supportive of the regime by 1943–1944, active opposition groups had very few members. The Bomb Plot only involved 22 out of 2000 generals, for example. Many in the army felt bound by their oath to Hitler.

■ The existence of the terror state: opposition during wartime meant people involved in resistance faced enormous risks, such as execution or indefinite imprisonment in **concentration camps**.

■ They acted too late: **conservatives**, for example, only started to resist the regime after the point when its power was secure.

■ Resistance did not in general involve a worked-out plan to remove the Nazis.

Simple essay style

Below is a sample Part (a) exam-style question. Use your own knowledge and the information on the opposite page to produce a plan for this question. Choose four general points, and provide three pieces of specific information to support each general point. Once you have planned your essay, write the introduction and conclusion for the essay. The introduction should list the points to be discussed in the essay. The conclusion should summarise the key points and justify which point was the most important.

How widespread was opposition to the Nazi regime during the Second World War?

Develop the detail

Below are a sample Part (a) exam-style question and a paragraph written in answer to this question. The paragraph contains a limited amount of detail. Annotate the paragraph to add additional detail to the answer.

'Opposition to the Nazi regime had no significant impact on civilian morale during the Second World War.' How far do you agree with this opinion?

Left-wing opposition to the Nazi regime failed to have a serious impact on civilian morale during the Second World War. Robert Uhrig established resistance cells. Other socialists organised in other localities. The communists also set up anti-Nazi groups to collect information. Nonetheless, these groups were largely ineffective. Nazi intelligence services were successful in breaking up left-wing groups. The success of Nazi intelligence agencies meant that left-wing groups were unable to get their message across to the public, and therefore these groups had little impact on civilian morale during the war.

How efficient was the Nazi war economy?

Fighting the war placed enormous strains on the German economy and labour force.

The German economy during the early part of the war

Early on in the war, Hitler sought to dramatically expand the German war economy and issued a series of **decrees** to increase war production. Between 1939 and 1941, German military expenditure doubled. By 1941, 55 per cent of the workforce was involved in war-related projects. Despite these efforts, however, German productivity was disappointing and below that of their enemies. Britain produced twice as many aircraft as Germany in 1941 and the USSR 2600 more tanks. The chaotic organisation of the Nazi state hindered economic efficiency, as the various bodies responsible did not co-ordinate effectively. During the war, the Office of the Four Year Plan, various parts of the SS, the Ministry of Economics, the Ministry of Armaments and the armed forces all had responsibility for armaments production whilst, at a local level, the powerful **Gauleiters** often interfered with economic plans.

The appointment of Speer

To try to resolve these difficulties, Fritz Todt, head of the Ministry of Armaments, simplified the production of armaments in January 1942. Industry was now directed to increase productivity. Hitler sought to further improve matters by appointing his trusted confidant, Albert Speer, as Minister of Munitions in February 1942 following Todt's death. In September 1943, Speer's powers were extended when he was given responsibility for all industry and raw materials as Minister for Armaments and Production.

Speer took a number of actions including:

- developing the work of Todt in establishing a Central Planning Board to co-ordinate economic organisation, while also giving industry more freedom to develop
- trying to exclude the military from economic planning
- encouraging the employment of women (with limited success)
- using concentration camp prisoners as labour
- preventing the conscription of skilled workers
- deploying production lines
- encouraging the standardisation of armaments and establishing an Armaments Commission to oversee this.

Speer had considerable success, as ammunition production rose by 97 per cent, tank production by 25 per cent and total arms production by 59 per cent. Between 1942 and 1944 German war production trebled. Raw materials were also used more efficiently and productivity per worker increased by 60 per cent in munitions.

The shortcomings of Goering

One of the reasons why the Nazi war economy performed so badly was the shortcomings of Goering. Hitler had appointed Goering as **Plenipotentiary** for the Office of the Four Year Plan in 1936. Consequently, he gave Goering almost limitless authority over the economy. However, Goering made strategic mistakes in economic planning. For example, he refused to introduce mass production into the aircraft industry and he wasted resources producing **ersatz** goods when cheaper imports were available. From 1939, Goering's morphine addiction was so severe that he was unable to work effectively. He spent most of the war neglecting his duties, collecting art from conquered territories, binging on chocolate, shopping in Paris, and fuelling his drug addiction.

Eliminate irrelevance

(a)

Below are a sample Part (a) exam-style question and a paragraph written in answer to this question. Read the paragraph and identify parts of the paragraph that are not directly relevant to the question. Draw a line through the information that is irrelevant and justify your deletions in the margin.

'The German war economy was inefficient for the duration of the Second World War.' How far do you agree with this opinion?

In the early part of the Second World War there is no doubt that the German war economy was highly inefficient. There were some successes. For example, between 1939 and 1941 Germany military expenditure doubled, and by 1941, 55 per cent of the workforce was involved in military production of some sort. However, in spite of these efforts, German productivity lagged behind the productivity of Britain and Russia. The British were able to produce twice as many aircraft in 1941 as the Germans. This was a major embarrassment to Herman Goering, the Chief of the Luftwaffe, who had staked his reputation on the success of his airforce. Additionally, the Russians were able to produce many more tanks than the Germans. However, it should be noted that, before June 1941, Russia and Germany were not at war, having signed a non-aggression pact in 1939. This lack of productivity can be explained by the chaotic organisation of the Nazi war economy, which was characterised by competing, overlapping organisations with no effective co-ordination. Historians have called this type of organisation 'polycratic'. In this way, the German war economy was certainly inefficient in the early years of the Second World War, because German productivity lagged behind that of other major powers.

Developing an argument

Below are a sample Part (a) exam-style question, a list of key points to be made in the essay, and a paragraph from the essay. Read the question, the plan, and the sample paragraph. Rewrite the paragraph in order to develop an argument. Your paragraph should explain why the factor discussed in the paragraph is either the most significant factor or less significant than another factor.

To what extent were the inadequacies of the German war economy primarily due to Hitler's refusal to mobilise women?

Key points:

- Hitler's refusal to mobilise women
- The inefficiency of the Nazi state
- Allied bombing raids
- Shortages of labour and raw materials

Sample paragraph

One reason for the inadequacies of the German war economy was the inefficiency of the Nazi state. For example, at the outbreak of war, in 1939, there were several agencies that had control of the Nazi economy. The Todt Organisation was responsible for the production of armaments, as was the Minister of Armaments and the Office of the Four Year Plan. The Ministry of Economics, under Walther Funk, was responsible for the general economic policy of Germany, as was the Office of the Four Year Plan under Hermann Goering. The SS was responsible for the economies of the newly conquered territories. Consequently, it had control of large reserves of manpower and raw materials. Yet, there was no co-ordinating body to ensure that the SS, the Office of the Four Year Plan, the Ministry of Economics, the Todt Organisation, or the Ministry of Armaments worked together. In this way, the inefficiency of the Nazi state played a role in the inadequacies of the German war economy, because it made it impossible to administer the economy effectively.

The failures of the war economy

Although German production levels increased, Germany was still out-produced by the USA and crucially also by the Soviet Union. In the end, despite the improvements in efficiency that Speer had put in place, the failures of the war economy contributed to Germany's defeat. There are a number of reasons for this:

■ The state remained chaotic with some Gauleiters and the SS often acting against economic efficiency.

■ Labour shortages held the economy back:
  – Unlike in the Soviet Union, Britain and the USA, women were not fully mobilised.
  – There was a heavy reliance on foreign workers (of whom there were 6.4 million by 1942). These were often little more than badly treated and underfed slave labourers; as a result their productivity was 60–80 per cent lower than that of the average German worker.

■ Shortages of raw materials, such as coal and oil, were a problem of the war economy: the production of ersatz materials did not fully compensate for this.

■ Germany needed the raw materials of the countries that they conquered in order to fight a major war, but the destructive manner of their conquest was not conducive to the effective exploitation of these resources. The SS were often more preoccupied with implementing racial policy than effectively organising the territory that they held and plunder did not amount to efficient economic organisation.

■ Supply of some materials, such as iron ore and magnesium, did improve as other countries were overrun but in the Soviet Union, Stalin's **scorched earth policy** hindered the Nazis: in the Donbass region of the Ukraine, the output of Soviet coal mines was only five per cent of pre-war levels in 1942, for example.

■ Allied bombing reduced the capacity of the German economy to expand further: industry was targeted and the Germans had to divert crucial resources towards **defensive** measures.

Women workers

Nazi ideology and policy had encouraged women to stay at home and raise children. Despite this, 52 per cent of German women worked at the time of the outbreak of war. The failure to actually conscript women or organise a campaign to increase their participation, combined with the already fairly high level of female employment meant that increasing the labour supply via the use of women workers did not really occur.

Spectrum of significance

Below are a sample Part (a) exam-style question and a list of general points which could be used to answer the question. Use your own knowledge and the information on the opposite page to reach a judgement about the importance of these general points to the question posed. Write numbers on the spectrum below to indicate their relative importance. Having done this, write a brief justification of your placement, explaining why some of these factors are more important than others. The resulting diagram could form the basis of an essay plan.

Why was the Nazi war economy so inefficient during the Second World War?

1. The inefficiencies of the Nazi state
2. Hitler's refusal to mobilise women
3. Shortages of raw materials
4. Shortages of labour
5. Allied bombing raids
6. The shortcomings of Goering

Very important ⟵⟶ Less important

Introducing an argument

Below are a sample Part (a) exam-style question, a list of key points to be made in the essay, and a simple introduction and conclusion for the essay. Read the question, the plan, and the introduction and conclusion. Rewrite the introduction and the conclusion in order to develop an argument.

Why was the Nazi war economy so inefficient during the Second World War?

Key points
- The inefficiencies of the Nazi state
- Hitler's refusal to mobilise women
- Shortages of raw materials
- Shortages of labour
- Allied bombing raids
- The shortcomings of Goering

Introduction

> There were a number of key reasons why the Nazi war economy was so inefficient during the Second World War. These were the inefficiencies of the Nazi state, Hitler's refusal to mobilise women, shortages of raw materials, shortages of labour, allied bombing raids and the shortcomings of Goering.

Conclusion

> There were a number of key reasons why the Nazi war economy was so inefficient during the Second World War. The most important reason was inefficiencies of the Nazi state. This played a more significant role than all of the other factors.

The persecution of the Jews

Origins

Europe had a long history of Christian anti-Semitism. While in most parts of Europe **the Enlightenment** period had seen improvements in the rights of Jews, in certain areas, such as **Tsarist Russia**, Jews remained oppressed and **pogroms** occurred. At the turn of the twentieth century, old prejudices against Jews fused with new pseudo-scientific racial ideas and the idea that the Jews were racially inferior influenced **anti-Semitic** extremists. In Nazi Germany, the doctrine of Aryan racial supremacy had dangerous consequences for Jews and other people who did not fit into the Nazis' conception of a **master race**.

Victims of the Nazis, 1939–1945

- The Second World War caused more than 60 million deaths in total, including 26.6 million Soviet citizens.

- Around 6 million Jews died in the Holocaust (two-thirds of the Jewish population of Europe) along with around 250,000–500,000 Roma people and 15,000 homosexuals.

- Over 1 million people (primarily Jews) were murdered by the **Einsatzgruppen** and their local collaborators in Eastern Europe and the USSR.

- Some 3 million Soviet prisoners of war were murdered or starved to death.

Persecution in Europe – timeline

Year	Persecution affecting Jews	Persecution affecting other groups
1933	• 1 April – Boycott of Jewish shops • April – All Jews except war veterans removed from the civil service	• Political opponents of the Nazi regime held in concentration camps • Law for compulsory sterilisation of the mentally ill
1935	• September – The **Nuremberg Laws** banned 'intermarriage' and removed Jews from German citizenship	• **A-socials**, including the homeless and alcoholics, put in concentration camps
1936		• Himmler established a Reich Office for Combating Homosexuality: 50,000 German homosexuals were arrested
1938	• March – Violent attacks on Jews and Jewish property following **Anschluss**. 45,000 Austrian Jews forced to emigrate • November – **Kristallnacht**: anti-Jewish attacks on thousands of businesses and synagogues. Some 20,000 Jewish men sent to concentration camps • **Aryanisation** begins: Jewish property seized; Jews banned from German economic life	
1939	• January – The SS establish the Reich Central Office for Emigration to promote emigration of Jews out of Europe • September – Ghettos for Polish Jews established	• German Roma people sent to concentration camps in Poland and Germany • The 'euthanasia' programme, Aktion T4, against disabled and mentally ill people starts
1940	• The Madagascar Plan drawn up: a plan to move 4 million European Jews to live in Madagascar: the idea was eventually abandoned as impractical	• A group of Roma children were gassed in Buchenwald concentration camp
1941	• All Jews forced to wear the Star of David • June – Following the invasion of the Soviet Union, *Einsatzgruppen* and their local supporters carried out systematic massacres of Jews	
1942	• January – The Wannsee Conference: representatives of various party and state organisations agreed to the '**Final Solution**' • Spring – Death camps established at Auschwitz, Sobibor and Treblinka	
1943–1944	• Transportation of European Jews to death camps	

Support or challenge?

Below is a sample Part (a) exam-style question which asks how far you agree with a specific statement. Below this is a series of general statements which are relevant to the question. Using your own knowledge and the information on the opposite page decide whether these statements support or challenge the statement in the question and tick the appropriate box.

'The 'Final Solution' was the result of systematic planning from 1933.' How far do you agree with this opinion?

	SUPPORT	CHALLENGE
All Jews were removed from the civil service in 1933, except for veterans of the First World War.		
In 1935, the Nuremberg Laws removed citizenship from German Jews.		
In 1938, Kristallnacht resulted in the imprisonment of 20,000 Jews in concentration camps.		
In 1939, the SS established the Reich Central Office for Emigration.		
In 1940, the Nazis drew up the Madagascar Plan.		
In 1941, *Einsatzgruppen* were deployed throughout the conquered territories.		
In 1942, the Wannsee Conference co-ordinated the 'Final Solution'.		
In 1942, death camps were established at Auschwitz, Sobibor and Treblinka.		

Complete the Venn diagram

Use the information on the opposite page to add detail to the Venn diagram below. In the non-intersecting areas of the diagram, list aspects of Jewish persecution which were either legal, economic, or based on terror. In the intersecting areas of the diagram, note ways in which these methods of persecuting the Jews overlapped.

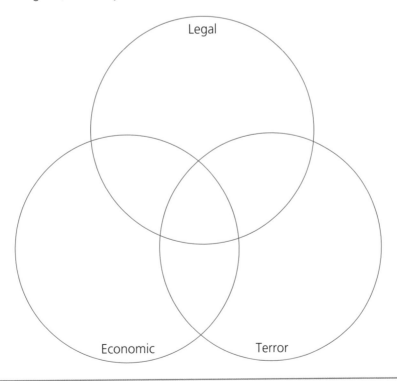

The causes of the 'Final Solution'

The role of Hitler

In Hitler's speeches, the 25 Points of the Nazi Party of 1920, and in *Mein Kampf* (1925), Hitler's view that Jews were not and should not be Germans was clear. His language could be considered **proto-genocidal**. Hitler's anti-Semitism was a core part of his world view. Hitler's ideas were the inspiration behind the ever-escalating anti-Semitism of his regime. It is also inconceivable that Hitler did not agree to the policy of the 'Final Solution' and indeed a diary entry of Himmler's indicates that, at a meeting to discuss the 'final solution of the Jewish question' in December 1941, Hitler authorised or ordered that Jews should be 'exterminated as partisans'. However, most historians do not believe that Hitler had a clear plan for the 'Final Solution' that pre-dated the war.

Cumulative radicalisation and the chaotic state

Another part of the explanation for the 'Final Solution' is that it was a consequence of the process of ever-growing extremism that occurred in the Third Reich as a result of the chaotic decision-making procedures. The chaos encouraged local initiatives and ideological radicalism. **Cumulative radicalisation** led to escalating action: German Jews were subject to restrictions and repression at the start of the war, but were not confined to ghettos. Polish Jews were then subject to the same measures and ordered into overcrowded ghettos ran by the SS. When Germany invaded the Soviet Union, *Einsatzgruppen*, who followed the army ensuring SS control, had wide-ranging instructions to eliminate opponents and massacres of Jews followed. These became systematic as the army moved eastwards and culminated in a policy of organised genocide in the death camp system.

The impact of the war

The 'Final Solution' developed in the context of war:

- The German invasion of Poland had created what the Nazis regarded as a problem: the Jewish population of Poland was large, around 3 million. Jews were forced into ghettos which were overcrowded and insanitary. When Jews from other parts of Europe started to be deported to the ghettos, the problem intensified.

- Fighting, particularly on the Eastern Front, was brutal and dehumanising.

- When invading areas of the Soviet Union, *Einsatzgruppen* carried out the first systematic massacres of the Holocaust: when the 'Final Solution' was planned, mass killings of Jews and some other groups, such as Roma people, were already occurring in the USSR.

- As the invasion of the Soviet Union put strains on the German war economy, the cost of feeding people in ghettos was considered too great.

- With the failure of the Madagascar Plan and the success of small-scale experiments with murder by gas, the plan for the 'Final Solution' was drawn up and executed: the systematic transportation to death camps of the entire Jewish population of Europe.

> **The *Einsatzgruppen***
>
> These were SS Death squads who followed the German army as Germany conquered Eastern Europe and the Soviet Union, carrying out mass killings of ideological and 'racial' enemies of the Nazis.

Conclusions

The Holocaust and the 'Final Solution' were inspired and authorised by Hitler, but there was not a clear blueprint to try to murder all of the Jews of Europe until after the invasion of the Soviet Union. The policy developed in the context of the war and the cumulative radicalisation of the Nazi state.

RAG – Rate the timeline

Below are a sample Part (a) exam-style question and a timeline. Read the question, study the timeline and, using three coloured pens, put a Red, Amber or Green star next to the events to show:

Red: Events and policies that have no relevance to the question
Amber: Events and policies that have some significance to the question
Green: Events and policies that are directly relevant to the question

1) To what extent was the chaotic nature of the Nazi regime the prime reason for the evolution of the 'Final Solution' in the years 1939–1945?

Now repeat the activity with the following questions:

2) 'The inefficient nature of the Nazi war economy was a result of the shortcomings of Goering.' How far do you agree with this opinion?

3) 'Widespread repression was unnecessary in Germany during the Second World War due to the high levels of civilian morale.' How far do you agree with this opinion?

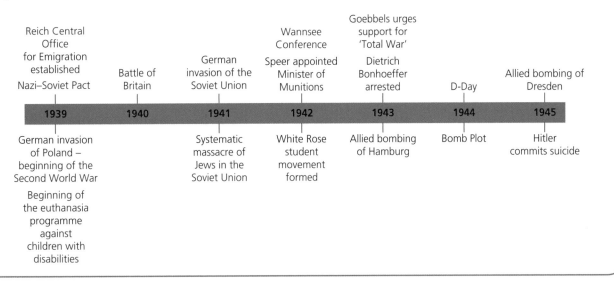

The flaw in the argument (a)

Below are a sample Part (a) exam-style question and a conclusion written in answer to this question. The conclusion contains an argument, but there is a flaw in this argument. Use your knowledge of the topic to identify the flaw in the argument.

To what extent was the chaotic nature of the Nazi regime the prime reason for the evolution of the 'Final Solution' in the years 1939–1945?

> In conclusion, the chaotic nature of the Nazi regime cannot explain the evolution of the 'Final Solution' in the years 1939–1945. Rather, the 'Final Solution' was the last step in a carefully planned process that began with the boycott of Jewish shops in 1933. At every stage, the Nazis increased persecution of the Jews, from a one-day boycott in 1939, to a denial of citizenship in 1935, to state-sponsored emigration in 1938, to mass extermination in the middle of the war. The logical nature of the development of Nazi Jewish policy is a clear indication that Hitler had a definite plan for dealing with the Jews and that he carried out this plan during his time in power.

Exam focus

Below is a sample A grade Part (a) essay. Read it and the examiner comments around it.

'The chaotic nature of the Nazi government best explains the failure of Hitler's war economy.' How far do you agree with this opinion?

The introduction begins by defining two ways in which the Nazi war economy failed. The essay achieves a mark in Level 5 partly because it refers back to these definitions in the course of the essay, linking the different causes of failure to the two aspects of failure stated here.

Hitler's war economy failed in two main ways. First, it was unable to maximise the productivity of the German labour force. Secondly, it was never able to out-produce Britain, Russia or America. Clearly, the chaotic nature of the Nazi government explains the failures of Hitler's war economy prior to the appointment of Speer as Minister of Munitions in February 1942. However, after this, other factors, such as labour shortages, shortages of raw material, and Allied bombings, play a larger role in explaining the failures of the war economy, because Speer, in alliance with other senior Nazis, was largely able to rationalise the war economy.

This paragraph deals with the stated factor, but acknowledges that its significance changes over time. This shows a detailed and nuanced knowledge of the period.

The chaotic nature of Nazi government certainly explains the failure of Hitler's war economy up until January 1942. Between 1939 and 1942, Goering's Office of the Four Year Plan was largely responsible for the co-ordination of the war economy. However, Goering was never able to assert full authority over the economy. Indeed, in Hitler's polycratic state, Goering had to compete with Fritz Todt, Minister of Armaments, Heinrich Himmler, Head of the SS, Walther Funk, Minister of Economics, and, at a local level, Gauleiters. This structure was part of Hitler's attempt to protect his own position and ensure an efficient state through intense competition. However, in practice, the economy failed to perform. For example, in 1941, Britain produced twice as many aircraft as Germany. Equally, in the same year, Russia produced more tanks than Germany. In this way, the chaotic nature of Nazi government helps to explain the failure of the war economy because a lack of co-ordination led to poor productivity.

Here, the candidate balances the emphasis on the stated factor with a detailed counter-argument, showing that the chaotic nature of government cannot wholly explain the failure of the war economy. Indeed, the candidate challenges the premise of the question, arguing that Nazi government of the economy was not chaotic for the entirety of the war.

Nevertheless, after the appointment of Speer in 1942, there was a concerted effort to streamline economic decision making and boost productivity. Speer used his power to establish a Central Planning Board to co-ordinate economic production and set industry free from the Office of the Four Year Plan. Additionally, Speer excluded senior military officials, including Goering, from economic decision making. As a result, between 1942 and 1944, ammunition production rose by 97 per cent, tank production rose by 25 per cent, and total military production rose by 59 per cent. In this sense, Speer was able to help the Nazi economy succeed by vastly increasing its productivity. Even so, production remained below that of Britain, Russia and America and therefore, Speer's rationalisation was not sufficient to make the economy a success. In this way, although the Nazi economy continued to fail under Speer, it was not as a result of chaotic government because Speer had done a great deal to rationalise the economy.

The Nazi war economy never succeeded in maximising the productivity of the German labour force. This was due, in part, to Hitler's view of women, rather than the chaotic nature of government. Hitler believed that women should not be involved in industrial production. As a result, although 52 per cent of German women were working in September 1939, this number did not increase as the war progressed. Speer attempted to encourage the employment of women, but Hitler rejected this suggestion, knowing that part of the appeal of his government was its emphasis on the traditional role of women. As a result, the Nazi economy failed to mobilise its labour force because of Nazi ideology rather than chaos in government.

Another factor which led to the failure of Hitler's war economy was the lack of raw materials. The Nazis assumed that conquest would lead to an increasing supply of raw materials. However, in practice, the German war effort was highly destructive and therefore they destroyed many of the resources they had hoped to utilise. Additionally, the SS, who administered conquered territories, were more interested in implementing racial policy than developing an efficient economic organisation. Furthermore, Stalin instituted a scorched earth policy in the coal-rich Donbass region of the Ukraine. Consequently, the Nazis were unable to gain access to Soviet raw materials. In this way, the lack of raw materials led to the failure of the Nazi economy because, without access to raw materials, the Nazis were unable to out-produce their enemies.

Finally, allied bombings reduced the capacity of the German economy. The allies specifically targeted German industrial centres, with the goal of destroying industry, the lives of workers, and breaking workers' morale. Tens of thousands were killed in firestorms caused by allied bombing raids targeting Hamburg in 1943, and Dresden in 1945. In this way, the failure of Hitler's war economy was partially the result of allied bombing rather than the chaotic nature of Nazi government, because bombing destroyed German industry and German workers.

In conclusion, the chaotic nature of the Nazi government certainly explains the failure of the Nazi war economy in the period 1939 to 1941. After 1942, Speer did a great deal to rationalise government administration and boost productivity. Even so, the Nazi war economy was unable to maximise the productivity of the German workforce because of the Nazi attitude to women and allied bombing raids which destroyed the morale of workers. Additionally, the war economy was never able to out-produce its enemies, because of the lack of raw materials and the effectiveness of allied bombing.

This is a weaker paragraph, due to the fact that it only discusses the productivity of one group. This does not show the range of knowledge needed to score a mark high in Level 5. It could be improved by discussing foreign and slave labour.

This paragraph is well organised. It explains the lack of raw materials with reference to three distinct factors: the destructive nature of the German war effort, the SS, and Stalin's scorched earth policy. This shows good command of the material.

Again, this is a paragraph that is weak in terms of supporting evidence. The paragraph could be improved by adding statistics to illustrate the impact of the allied bombing raids.

The conclusion is consistent with the argument set out in the introduction, and refers back to the definition of failure used throughout the essay. This shows sustained analysis.

26/30

This essay achieves a mark in Level 5 because it contains sustained analysis, consistently arguing that the chaotic nature of Nazi government cannot fully explain the failure of Hitler's war economy. However, the essay achieves a mark low in Level 5 because a number of the paragraphs lack the level of detail expected at Level 5.

What makes a good answer?

You have now considered four sample A grade Part (a) essays. Use these essays to make a bullet-pointed list of the characteristics of an A grade Part (a) essay. Use this list when planning and writing your own practice exam essays.

Glossary

Aktion T4 The Nazi programme to kill mentally and physically ill and disabled people, which ran officially from 1939–1941, but which continued secretly afterwards. It resulted in the murder of more than 200,000 people. The programme was sometimes referred to as euthanasia, when it was in fact murder.

Allies (in the context of the First World War) Britain, Russia and France and their empires.

Anglo-French Agreement A 1904 agreement between Britain and France known as the Entente Cordiale. The agreement included settlement of various colonial and territorial disputes. Having historically been enemies, the Entente Cordiale saw the start of a co-operative relationship between the two countries. The Entente Cordiale was one of the agreements that formed the Triple Entente.

Anglo-Russian Entente A 1907 agreement between Britain and Russia, which resolved various disputes between the two countries over influence and control in Asia. The Anglo-Russian Entente was one of the agreements that formed the Triple Entente.

Annexation Where one country takes over and incorporates another. Annexations are forced but peaceful.

Anschluss The union of Germany and Austria.

Anti-Semitic Prejudiced views or hatred towards Jewish people or the Jewish religion, or a measure that discriminates against Jews.

Appeasement Attempting to resolve a dispute by making concessions to an aggressor in order to try to avoid war.

Armistice An agreement to stop fighting at the end of a war.

Aryanisation To make Aryan. In Nazi Germany this term usually referred to the confiscation of Jewish property after 1938: non-Jewish Germans were given Jewish homes, businesses, etc.

A-socials A term applied to those in Germany who did not fit with the Nazi's conception of a unified national community, because of their unconventional life or perceived attitude to work. Beggars and tramps were labelled a-social, for example. A-socials were persecuted by the Nazis.

Austro-Hungarian Empire The Austro-Hungarian Empire existed from 1867 to 1918. Its capital was Vienna and Austria was the predominant power, although Hungary had considerable power over their territories. Both countries had colonial possessions, including large parts of the Balkans.

Autocrat Rule of one: a ruler of a country who holds all power.

Balance of power Keeping any one country from becoming excessively powerful.

Balkan Wars These conflicts in 1912 and 1913 destabilised peace in Europe. Countries including Serbia, Montenegro, Greece, Bulgaria and Romania fought against the Ottoman Empire and among themselves for territorial control of the Balkan region. The Balkan Wars saw the Ottomans largely forced out of Europe, and Serbia double in size.

Bamberg Conference A Nazi Party conference in 1926 at which Hitler's role as the single all-powerful leader of the movement was reinforced. In addition, Hitler defeated the left of the party to ensure that the party had a clearly right-wing agenda.

Battle of Britain An air battle between Britain and Germany in 1940. German and British fighter pilots fought in the skies above southern England. Hitler's aim was to try to force the British out of the war.

Battle of the Atlantic A battle in the Second World War between the German navy and Allied navies and airforces. The battle lasted for most of the duration of the war and centred around German attempts to disrupt and destroy convoys of supplies and soldiers across the Atlantic.

Bauhaus A modern school of design founded in Germany in 1919.

Bavaria Project A large historical research project investigating the lives of ordinary people in Bavaria 1933–1945. The project was led by Martin Broszat.

Bill of Rights A constitutional document that outlines the protected rights that people have within a state, for example, freedom of speech.

Blank Cheque A term used to express the significance of the unconditional backing that the Germans gave the Austrians during the July Crisis of 1914. The 'Blank Cheque' is argued by some to have encouraged the Austrians into aggressive action against Serbia.

Blitzkrieg 'Lightning war': the tactics of the German army when invading.

Block Wardens (in Nazi Germany) A person responsible for local level political supervision of their neighbourhood. Wardens would spread propaganda and spy on their neighbours.

Boer War 1899–1902 A conflict fought between the British Empire and the Boers who were Dutch settlers in Southern Africa. The Germans were supportive of the Boers during this conflict.

Bundesrat The federal council in the Second Reich. This body could initiate legislation.

Burgfriede A term used by Kaiser Wilhelm II at the start of the First World War to mean 'national truce': a term for the unity in the German political scene at the start of the war.

Cabaret A sometimes satirical art form practised in nightclubs, usually through the medium of dance and song.

Centrist A person whose political views are ideologically in the centre of politics, i.e. they do not lean particularly to the left or the right.

Checks and balances Parts of a constitution or political system that ensure that no one part of the system or one individual within it can have excessive power.

Collateral Something used to guarantee security such as for a loan or currency – for example, gold to guarantee paper money; property as collateral for a loan.

Concentration camp (in Nazi Germany) Camps where the Nazis held their opponents or others, such as racial minorities, who did not fit into their ideal for society.

Concordat An agreement signed between the Catholic Church and the government of any country.

Conservatives People or political movements who favour upholding traditional institutions, values and social classes.

Coup From *coup d'état*: the sudden, illegal overthrow of a government.

Cumulative radicalisation The process by which policies in Nazi Germany became ever more extreme.

Customs union A free trade area with a common external tariff.

D-Day The Allied invasion of Normandy in France on 6 June 1944. The invasion opened up a third front against the Nazis in Europe.

Decadence A culture of frivolity and indulgence. Decadence usually implies moral decline.

Decree An official order or law.

Defensive Action taken in order to avoid defeat or attack.

Demilitarised Removing or not allowing a military force from an area, for example in the Rhineland after the First World War.

Direct democracy A political arrangement in which people get a direct say in decisions about policies.

Dissolve (in the context of a parliament) To remove all members of a parliamentary body from their posts. Usually a new election is then called.

Eastern Front (in the First and Second World Wars) The front line between German / German-Austrian forces and Russian / Soviet forces.

Ebert–Groener Pact A pact agreed on 10 November 1918 between SPD leader Ebert and army general Groener after the Kaiser fled Germany. Groener agreed that the army would respect and defend the new government and in return Ebert agreed that the new government would leave the army and civil service of Germany unreformed, i.e. with their personnel and existing hierarchies intact.

Edelweiss Pirates An illegal youth group in Nazi Germany who were opposed to Nazi rule.

Einsatzgruppen SS Death squads who followed the German army as Germany conquered Eastern Europe and the Soviet Union carrying out mass killings of ideological and 'racial' enemies of the Nazis.

Encirclement When one country is surrounded by its enemies or competing powers.

Encyclical A letter from the Pope to all Roman Catholic bishops.

The Enlightenment An eighteenth-century cultural movement to improve knowledge and reform and advance society.

Enshrined Something that is protected or something that is given superior status in law.

Entrenched Something that is stable and secure.

Ersatz Substitute or replacement goods.

Expressionist Artistic works in which artists seek to reveal their personal emotional responses through, for example, use of vivid colour or exaggerated perspective.

Federal A political system where substantial power is held at regional level over areas such as education policy.

Final Solution The euphemistic term the Nazis used to refer to the Holocaust and death camps; they were, in Nazi terms, the 'final solution to the Jewish question'.

Franco-Russian Alliance A military alliance between France and Russia that lasted from 1894 to 1917. The Alliance formed part of the Triple Entente.

Freikorps Paramilitary (informal) groups of volunteer soldiers. In inter-war Germany these groups were often strongly nationalist and linked to extremist politics.

Front Area of combat in a war.

Fulfilment The term applied to Gustav Stresemann's foreign policy of meeting (fulfilling) Germany's international obligations, such as the payment of reparations, and involving Germany in international organisations and international affairs, while also seeking to renegotiate the terms of the Treaty of Versailles through, for example, the Dawes Plan.

Gauleiter A Nazi Party leader who was head of a regional party office or when the Nazis were in power, a region of Germany.

Gestapo The internal German secret police during the Nazi period.

Grand Coalition The coalition government formed in 1928 in Germany. The government included representatives from left and right and was headed by Chancellor Müller of the SPD. The government was the longest lived of the Weimar Republic.

Great Depression A sustained period of world-wide economic decline in the 1930s.

Great Powers The most dominant countries or empires in the world. Usually refers to European powers before the First World War.

Habeas corpus The right of a prisoner to challenge the basis of their incarceration, i.e. a person cannot be held for no reason and without an opportunity to respond to allegations.

Hegemony Having dominant power in an area.

High treason The crime of betraying your country or ruler. This crime is often punishable by death.

Hossbach meeting A 1937 meeting between Hitler, senior military figures and the foreign minister at which, according to the minutes of the meeting taken by Colonel Hossbach, Hitler determined upon wars of plunder in the east by 1939 and war with Britain and France by 1941. The meeting has often been interpreted as representing a new radical phase in Hitler's foreign policy.

Hottentot election 1907 A German election held after the Kaiser dissolved the Reichstag. The Centre Party and the SPD had opposed the government's imperial policy in Africa and in the subsequent election this was the biggest issue. The election resulted in an improved standing for pro-imperial conservative policies. Hottentot is a European word for southern Africans common in the late nineteenth and early twentieth centuries.

Imperialists Those who pursue a policy to create and maintain an empire. Imperialism also relates to the ideas that might be used to justify such a policy.

Inflation Occurs when prices rise and the amount that can be purchased with each unit of a currency reduces: the value of a currency declines in an inflationary situation.

Intentionalist A historical viewpoint that places weight on the role that individual intentions have upon events. Intentionalists believe that individuals have great capacity to shape history.

Isolationist A policy in which a country keeps out of involvement in foreign affairs.

Junkers The old elite of Germany; the dominant social group in the Second Reich. *Junkers* were aristocratic landowners from Prussia who occupied most of the senior positions in the army, civil service and politics in the Second Reich.

Kapp Putsch An attempt to take over the government of the Weimar Republic by members of the Freikorps and civil servant Wolfgang Kapp, following an attempt to disband part of the Freikorps in line with the requirements of the Treaty of Versailles. The main leader of the Putsch was army general Lüttwitz, but Kapp was lined up to be Chancellor. The Putsch temporarily succeeded and the government was forced out of Berlin for a number of days. The Putsch was defeated following a massive general strike in opposition to it in Berlin.

Kristallnacht The Night of Broken Glass: an orchestrated Nazi attack on Jewish property and businesses on 9–10 November 1938.

League of Nations An international organisation of nation-states formed after the First World War with the aim of promoting disarmament and world peace.

Lebensraum Literally 'living space'. Refers to the German aim of pursuing territorial expansion in Eastern Europe.

Left-wing Political beliefs that promote the creation of a more equal society.

Left-wing underground Left-wing political groups operating secretly during times of repression.

Legislation Laws.

Liberalism A political ideology which focuses on individual freedom as the fundamental value of political life.

Lobbied Tried to convince a political figure of the merits of a cause or argument.

Low Countries Belgium, Holland and Luxembourg.

Mandate The right to do something, particularly in politics. Sometimes a mandate is conferred after a vote or election.

Mark A unit of German currency.

Master race (in racist ideology) A supposedly superior racial group.

Megalomaniac A person who tries to accumulate ever more power.

Militaristic Something that glorifies or promotes the military.

Mobilise Organising to fight a war.

Munich Putsch An attempt by the Nazis to seize control of the German state.

Nationalised A process by which ownership of a business is transferred to public or state ownership.

Nationalist politics Politics which seek to glorify or expand the nation.

Nazification (usually in relation to German institutions) To extend Nazi control via, for example, displaying Nazi symbols, the swearing of oaths of allegiance to Hitler, the promotion of Nazi values.

Nazi–Soviet Pact A non-aggression pact signed on 28 August 1939 between Nazi Germany and the Soviet Union at the instigation of Germany. The pact also involved an agreement to carve up Poland between the two countries. Hitler breached the agreement by invading the USSR in June 1941.

Newsreels Filmed news reports shown in cinemas.

Night of the Long Knives The name given to the occasion on 30 June 1934 when Hitler and members of the SS arrested and murdered Röhm and other SA leaders and the SA was brought under SS control. A number of other political opponents of the Nazis, like von Schleicher, were also murdered. On the Night of the Long Knives, Hitler removed the threat to his position that the SA represented and consolidated his position with the army and his conservative supporters.

November criminals The term applied by the German right to the politicians who had signed the armistice on 11 November 1918. The term suggested that these people had betrayed Germany, when in reality they were neither to blame for Germany's defeat and nor did they have any real choice but to sign the agreement.

Nuremberg Laws Anti-Semitic Nazi laws introduced in 1935 which defined who the Nazis considered to be Jewish, banned future inter-marriage between Jews and 'Aryan' Germans and deprived Jews of German citizenship.

Nuremberg Trials International tribunals held in the German city of Nuremberg in 1945–1946 in which senior figures of the Nazi regime were tried for war crimes.

Obersalzberg A mountain in southern Germany overlooking Salzburg in Austria on which Hitler had a holiday home.

Operation Bagration A huge Soviet military offensive in 1944 in Eastern Europe.

Oratory The skill of speech-making.

Ottoman Empire A middle eastern and European empire ruled by Turkey that lasted from the thirteenth to the twentieth century.

Passive resistance Resisting a government via peaceful actions.

Patronage (in politics) The power to bestow favours or jobs on others. For example, part of the Kaiser's power of patronage was his power to appoint and dismiss the Chancellor of Germany.

Pearl Harbor A US naval base in the Pacific attacked by Japan in December 1941.

Personal rule Referring to a period when an autocrat dominates the political scene. The term has been used to describe periods of Charles I's and Kaiser Wilhelm II's rule.

Phoney war Where a war has been declared but no fighting occurs.

Plebiscite A democratic vote on a single issue. Can also be called a referendum.

Plenipotentiary A person who has full powers over an area of policy, for example Goering over the Office of the Four Year Plan.

Plurality Where there is a diverse range of interests and political groups.

Pogroms Massacres of Jews in Europe. The term pogroms is particularly associated with massacres committed in Tsarist Russia.

Polarisation (in a political context) A process whereby the political scene divides between the extreme left and the extreme right.

Politics from above The impact that those in the elite have on politics.

Politics from below The impact that ordinary people or political movements representing ordinary people have on politics.

Polycratic (polycracy) Many centres of power: in a state, power is shared between different sections of the state. These sections may be in competition with one another for power.

Pressure group An organised group that tries to influence government policy in a specific area.

Progressive A belief in social progress or liberal reform.

Progressive taxation Taxation that distributes resources from richer people to poorer people.

Proportional representation An electoral system in which seats allocated in parliament correspond exactly or very closely to the way in which people vote, i.e. if 10 per cent of voters vote for a party, then that party receives 10 per cent of the seats in parliament.

Protectionist An economic policy in which tariffs (taxes or fees) on imports are high in order to protect domestic producers and prevent them being undercut by cheaper goods from abroad.

Protective custody A euphemistic name for the arrest and detention of political and 'social' enemies of Nazi Germany.

Proto-genocidal An act or sentiment that encourages genocide or makes genocide more likely.

Prussia The largest and most powerful German state in the Second Reich. Before 1871, an independent state. Abolished in 1945.

Punitive Harsh.

Red Army The army of the Soviet Union.

Referenda Democratic votes on a single issue. Can also be called a plebiscite.

Rentenmark The German currency introduced in 1923 to replace the weak currency of the inflationary years.

Reparations Money or goods extracted from a losing country blamed for causing a war to compensate the victors for war costs and damage.

Resistance cells Secret groups who opposed the Nazi government.

Rote Kappelle Literally, the Red Orchestra. The term which German intelligence services used to refer to communist resistance networks during the Nazi era.

Sammlungspolitik 'Bringing together politics': von Bülow's policy of trying to unite conservative and centrist forces in the Second Reich in order to gain Reichstag support for his government and restrict the influence of socialists.

Schutzstaffel (SS) This organisation started off in the 1920s as Hitler's personal bodyguard, but expanded to become the main agents of terror in Nazi Germany. The SS were fiercely loyal to Hitler and his ideas. By 1934, the SS were rivals to the SA as the primary enforcers of Nazism. The SS were led by Heinrich Himmler and were responsible for repression and death camps in occupied territories in Eastern Europe during the Second World War.

Scorched earth policy A policy by which an advancing or retreating army or political power destroys land and infrastructure in their wake.

Sicherheitsdienst (SD) The intelligence agency of the SS.

Siegfriede Literally, Victory Peace. The term for the aims of those in Germany in the First World War who sought territorial expansion and European domination.

Socialism A political ideology which advocates the collective ownership of property and industry.

Social revolution A revolution in which the social order (i.e. existing class relations) is overturned. The term can also be used to refer to revolutionary changes in a society's attitudes.

SOPADE The term for The Social Democratic Party of Germany (SDP) in exile.

Sovereign The source of ultimate power within a state.

Soviets Workers' councils.

Soviet Union A Russian-dominated communist state in Eastern Europe and Asia.

Spanish flu pandemic A devastating outbreak of flu that occurred at the end of the First World War.

Spartacist League A communist affiliated political group in the Weimar Republic. Spartacists placed greater weight on the need for revolutions to have popular support than did Lenin, communist leader of the Soviet Union.

SPD The Social Democratic Party of Germany. The main left-wing party in Germany.

Sphere of influence An area over which a powerful state has de facto control or a strong influence.

Sportpalast 'Sports palace': a venue in Berlin for winter sports that doubled as a huge meeting hall, often used in Nazi Germany for speeches and rallies.

'Stab in the back myth' The right-wing myth that Germany only lost the First World War because of the revolution of autumn 1918 and because she was betrayed by socialists, communists and liberal politicians. In reality, Germany had already essentially lost the war before the revolution occurred.

Strength Through Joy A Nazi organisation which provided enhanced leisure opportunities for workers. Hikes and subsidised excursions to events like the opera were laid on for many, whilst a few benefited from Baltic cruises. The activities of the organisation were often used as propaganda to promote the benefits of the regime.

Structuralist A theory of history in which social, political and economic structures primarily determine the development of history. Examples of these structures include class and economics.

***Sturmabteilung* (SA)** 'Storm detachment'. The private army of the Nazi Party who attacked their political opponents and protected Nazis during their political meetings. Members of the SA were sometimes referred to as 'brownshirts', as this item was part of their uniform. Members of the organisation were usually ex-soldiers or unemployed young men. The head of the SA, Ernst Röhm, hoped to see the SA replace the traditional German army, but Röhm was killed during the Night of the Long Knives, partly in order to appease those in the army concerned about the SA's activities. Subsequently the SA was subordinated to the SS.

Tariff Law A German law of 1902 which restored agricultural tariffs to 1892 levels. The measure was a compromise, in that it reflected the demands of German conservatives that tariffs be raised in order to protect domestic landowners and farmers, but the increase in tariffs fell far short of the levels that the conservatives had demanded.

Teutonic Knight A medieval Germanic order of crusading knights.

Thesis A theory or interpretation.

Third Naval Law A German law of 1906 which involved the construction of six large warships.

Totalitarian A dictatorial system of government in which all power is centralised by the state and the state controls all aspects of life.

Treason Criminal betrayal of one's country.

Treaty of Versailles The peace treaty between the British and French Empires, the United States and their allies with Germany negotiated at the end of the First World War and signed on 28 June 1919.

Triple Alliance The term given to the alliances and agreements that existed between Germany, Austria–Hungary and Italy prior to the First World War.

Triple Entente The term given to the alliances and agreements that existed between the Russian, French and British Empires prior to the First World War.

Tsarist Russia The Russian Empire during the era that it was ruled by the Tsars (Emperors).

Universal suffrage Everyone having the vote.

USPD The Independent Socialist Party of Germany: a radical socialist party of the Second Reich and Weimar Germany.

USSR The Union of Soviet Socialist Republics: the official name for the Soviet Union (see page 110).

V1 and V2 rockets Missiles used by the Germans in the Second World War.

Veto To exercise the power to block a law or similar measure.

Volksgemeinschaft A 'people's community': a Nazi concept entailing the unity of all members of the 'racial' community who adhered to Nazi ideology. The Nazis aimed to create a unified *Volksgemeinschaft* in Germany.

Vote of no-confidence A parliamentary vote on whether the government or prime minister has the support of the parliament to continue in office. In some situations losing such a vote would force a prime minister out of office.

Wall Street Crash A stock market crash that started in October 1929, when the value of the stocks and shares on the US stock market in Wall Street, New York plunged as people sold off their investments. The value of shares had been inflated by a credit boom and the crash saw many bankrupted. The crash was one cause of the Great Depression of the 1930s.

War bonds Bought by citizens or businesses during wartime from the government to assist with the costs of the war: in effect, people lend the government money.

Wehrmacht The German armed forces, particularly of 1935–1945 and particularly the army.

Wehrwirtschaft War economy.

Weltpolitik 'World politics': the German policy developed from the mid-1890s of seeking enhanced power and status in Europe and around the world through colonial and military expansion.

Withered arm A small or shrunken arm with limited strength resulting from disability, illness or old age.

Working class Those who sell their labour to make money and do not own property or capital. The term usually refers to those who work in manual labour.

Timeline

1871 Prussia's victory in the Franco-Prussian War (1870–1871) leads to the unification of Germany

1888 Wilhelm II succeeds to the German throne

1905 Beginning of the First Moroccan Crisis

Creation of the Schlieffen Plan

1906 Third Naval Law

1907 Hottentot election

1908 Bosnian Crisis

1911 Second Moroccan Crisis

1912 German Imperial War Council meets

1913 Army Bill

Bethmann Hollweg loses a vote of no-confidence in the Reichstag

1914 Archduke Franz Ferdinand murdered

Germany offers Austria a 'Blank Cheque'

Outbreak of the First World War

The production of the September Programme

1916 Creation of the 'Silent Dictatorship'

1918 Outbreak of revolution in Germany

Abdication of Kaiser Wilhelm II

Declaration of the Republic

Ebert–Groener Pact

Armistice

1919 Ebert elected President

Spartacist uprising

Weimar constitution adopted

Treaty of Versailles signed

1920 Kapp Putsch

Support for pro-Weimar parties slumps to 45%

1921 Hitler becomes Führer of the Nazi Party

1923 Hyperinflation Crisis

Munich Putsch

1924 Dawes Plan

1925 Hindenburg elected President

1926 Germany admitted to the League of Nations

1928 Reichstag election: 76% of voters support pro-Weimar parties, the Nazis gain 2.6% of the vote

1929 Young Plan

Wall Street Crash

1932 Hindenburg wins the presidential election

(July) Reichstag election: Nazis gain 37% of the vote, becoming the largest party in the Reichstag

(November) Reichstag election: Nazi share of the vote declines to 32%

1933 Hitler appointed as Chancellor

Reichstag Fire

Dachau opened

Boycott of Jewish shops

Enabling Act

All political parties, except for the Nazis, disbanded

Concordat agreed with the Roman Catholic Church

1934 Night of the Long Knives

Plebiscite on merging the chancellery with the presidency

1935 Saar plebiscite

Nuremberg Laws passed

1936 Remilitarisation of the Rhineland

Creation of the Four Year Plan Organisation

Reich Office for Combating Homosexuality established

1937 *With Burning Concern* published

Hossbach meeting

1938 *Anschluss*

Kristallnacht

1939 Reich Central Office for Emigration established

Nazi–Soviet Pact

German invasion of Poland – beginning of the Second World War

Beginning of the Aktion T4 programme

1940 Battle of Britain

1941 German invasion of the Soviet Union

Systematic massacre of Jews in the Soviet Union

1942 Wannsee Conference

Speer appointed Minister of Munitions

1943 Allied bombing of Hamburg

1944 D-Day

Bomb Plot

1945 Allied bombing of Dresden

Hitler commits suicide

Nuremberg Trials

Answers

Section 1

Page 5, Complete the paragraph: suggested answer

The role of the Kaiser within the constitution of the Second Reich was evidence that the constitution was fundamentally undemocratic in nature. For example, **the Kaiser, without reference to the German people, could appoint the Chancellor and dissolve the Reichstag. The Kaiser was never elected and yet he was President of the Bundesrat and Commander-in-Chief of the Armed Forces. Therefore, the army was accountable to him alone and could not be controlled by the democratically elected Reichstag. Consequently, the government and army leadership were dominated by conservatives who favoured the interests of the Prussian aristocracy over those of the people more generally.** In this way, the role of the Kaiser indicates that the constitution of the Second Reich was fundamentally undemocratic because the Kaiser had great power which was unaccountable to the German people.

Page 5, Eliminate irrelevance

The Reichstag, or Parliament, was clearly the most democratic element of the constitution of the Second Reich, ~~which created a federal state~~. The Reichstag was designed ~~by Bismarck following Prussia's victory in the Franco-Prussian War~~, to give the German people a voice in the German government. ~~Otto von Bismarck himself was of Prussian origin, and therefore favoured the Prussians~~. The Reichstag was elected by all men over the age of 25 and had the power to reject, accept and amend any law. ~~Prior to the creation of the constitution, Germany had been little more than a customs union dominated by Prussia~~. However, there were limits to the power of the Reichstag. For example, the German army was accountable to the Kaiser only and therefore the elected representatives in the Reichstag could exercise no control over the army. Overall, the Reichstag is evidence that the constitution of the Second Reich was not fundamentally undemocratic in nature because, through control of the Reichstag, the German people could affect legislation. However, this democratic aspect of the constitution was deliberately limited and therefore it is impossible to argue that the constitution of the Second Reich was wholly democratic.

Page 9, Spot the mistake

The paragraph does not get into Level 4 because, although the examples are focused on the question, they lack specific detail.

Page 9, Develop the detail: suggested answer

One reason for the rise in support of the Social Democratic Party (SPD) was Germany's economic modernisation. For example, Germany experienced a lot of economic growth and the creation of new industries. **Between 1890 and 1914, the German economy expanded at a rate of around 4.5 per cent a year. For example, coal production almost doubled in the years to the First World War. Furthermore, Daimler and Diesel began producing automobiles and AEG and Siemens developed new electrical products**. At the same time, Germany became, for the first time in its history, an industrial economy. **Indeed, the contribution made by German industry rose from 33 per cent of GNP to 42 per cent in 1914**. This led to urbanisation – **by 1910 Cologne, Hamburg and Munich all had populations in excess of half a million** – and poor living standards, which in turn led to class tensions **between the growing working class and the *Junker* elite, who were determined to maintain their dominant position in German society**. Therefore, one reason for the rise in support of the SPD was economic modernisation, because it led to a rise in class tensions and consequently the popularity of left-wing political parties.

Page 19, The flaw in the argument

The argument is flawed because, although the Kaiser enjoyed considerable power from 1900 to 1914, following 1916, the Kaiser himself was sidelined by the 'silent dictatorship' of the military generals.

Section 2

Page 27, Summarise the interpretation

Source 1 does not support the view that the First World War came about because of German aggression. Instead, it argues that the decision to occupy Bosnia and Herzegovina led to war in 1914 because it showed a new willingness on the part of the Austrians to confront Pan-Serbian nationalism, which increased tensions in the area.

Source 2 argues that the Moroccan and Bosnian Crises did not fatally damage European peace, but did reveal worrying tendencies in German foreign policy. In this sense, Source 2 does not attribute the war to German aggression, but does note that German foreign policy had increased tensions.

Source 3 argues that the crises between 1900 and 1914 pushed many European statesmen to the conclusion that war was the only way of solving Europe's problems. Therefore, it does not single out German aggression as the primary cause of the war in Europe.

Page 31, Write the question: suggested answer

How far do you agree that 'the German government … wilfully turned the Balkan crisis of 1914 into a world war'?

How far do you agree that 'the concept of the window of opportunity' in the minds of German statesmen during the July Crisis of 1914 was the key cause of the First World War?

Section 3

Page 39, Complete the paragraph: suggested answer

One feature of the Weimar Constitution which was designed to guarantee stable government was Article 48. This article could be invoked by the President at times of emergency. Essentially, Article 48 gave the President the power to rule by decree in an emergency. This power was subject to the Reichstag. In practice, this meant that the Reichstag needed to authorise the use of Article 48, and that the Reichstag could review the use of Article 48 by overturning any emergency decrees that the President issued. **In this way, the Weimar constitution was not too democratic to ensure stable government because features such as Article 48 allowed the President, with the support of the Reichstag, to ensure the stability of the government in a time of crisis.**

Page 41, Develop the detail: suggested answer

There was much dissatisfaction with the Weimar constitution from the right wing of German politics. For example, the *Junkers*, **who had enjoyed considerable power in the Second Reich**, were excluded from some branches of government, **such as the Reichsrat**. Equally, conservative political parties, **such as the DVP**, opposed the Weimar constitution **because they favoured a constitutional monarchy**. Additionally, industrialists and business owners objected to the Weimar constitution **because of the welfare rights and trade union rights that it guaranteed to the workers**. Also, the democratic nature of the constitution concerned businessmen **because it gave power to the working class, who formed the majority of the population**. In this way, the Weimar constitution did not enjoy the majority of support from the right wing because there were concerns that it was too democratic and gave too much power to the workers.

Page 43, Eliminate irrelevance

One way in which defeat in the First World War did undermine the stability of Weimar Germany in the period 1919 to 1924 was the association between the new government and the 'November Criminals'. ~~The war had been caused by many factors, including the rivalry between Great Powers and the arms race.~~ German generals protected themselves from public criticism by alleging that they were betrayed by politicians who forced them to accept the terms of the armistice and later betrayed Germany by accepting reparations and full responsibility for the outbreak of the First World War. ~~German generals had taken over the running of the government in 1916, forming the 'Silent Dictatorship' which sidelined Wilhelm II from his own government.~~ Consequently, democratic politicians who had established the Weimar constitution were labelled the 'November Criminals' by their opponents in order to discredit the new democracy. ~~However, it was wrong to criticise German politicians because, as Fritz Fischer has argued, Germany was indeed responsible for the First World War.~~ In this way, the association between the Weimar Republic and defeat in the First World War undermined the stability of German democracy because, from the very beginning, democratic politicians were considered criminals who had betrayed their own country.

Page 45, Spot the mistake

The paragraph does not get into Level 4 because, although the examples are relevant to the question, their relevance is implicit as the candidate has written a narrative of left-wing revolt without drawing clear links between these revolts and the question.

Page 47, Eliminate irrelevance

Reparations were a major economic threat to the stability of the Weimar Republic in the period 1919 to 1924. The Treaty of Versailles stipulated that Germany had to pay reparations for the damage caused in the First World War. ~~Germany had lost the war as a result of economic problems and poor leadership.~~ In 1921, the total amount of reparations was set at 269 billion gold marks. In order to pay reparations and keep their economy afloat, the German government began to print money. By 1923, 300 paper mills and 150 printing presses worked day and night to create paper currency, leading to hyperinflation. ~~This was the opposite of the economic problems that affected Germany at the end of the 1920s, when the Wall Street Crash led to a Depression.~~ As a result, the mark became almost valueless. For example, in April 1919, 12 marks were needed to buy $1. However, by December 1923, 4.2 trillion marks were needed to buy $1. Consequently, the economic crisis led to the eradication of the savings of many Germans. ~~Fortunately, the Dawes Plan of 1924 agreed staged repayments of the reparations bill, and massive American loans which diffused the situation, decreasing tensions within Germany.~~ In this way, economic crisis led to political instability as the German public blamed their government for the decrease in their standard of living.

Page 47, Develop the detail: suggested answer

The Ruhr crisis shows the interrelation of political and economic problems which destabilised the Weimar

Republic. The crisis was caused by the failure of Germany to meet its reparation payments, **which in 1921 were set at 269 billion gold marks**. As a result, France and Belgium invaded the Ruhr, **an industrial region in Germany**, determined to seize reparations by force. The German government, **led by President Ebert**, resisted the invasion **by initiating a policy of passive resistance, whereby German workers went on strike rather than co-operate with the foreign invaders**. As a result, there was an economic crisis, **as the government lost revenue due to the strike and due to the fact that it paid the wages of the striking workers**. The Ruhr crisis led to hyperinflation and the value of the mark dropped **from 12 marks to the dollar in April 1919, to 4.2 trillion marks to the dollar in December 1923**. Thus, the political crisis of a foreign invasion led to the economic crisis of hyperinflation, both of which destabilised the Weimar Republic by demonstrating the weakness of the new government.

Page 51, The flaw in the argument

The argument is flawed because the majority of evidence provided in the paragraph contradicts the argument stated at the beginning.

Section 4

Page 57, Eliminate irrelevance

One of the reasons for the success of the Nazi movement in the period 1929 to 1932 was Nazi ideology. German nationalism appealed to many German people in the wake of the Wall Street Crash, ~~which was not the cause of the Great Depression, but was a catalyst,~~ and also following Germany's humiliating defeat in the First World War. Nazi nationalism asserted that Germany should be strong, and that all German-speaking peoples should be united in one state. Nazi nationalism also repudiated the terms of the Treaty of Versailles. ~~The Treaty of Versailles was given this name because it was signed in the Palace of Versailles, in France.~~ Social Darwinism, the notion that the fittest survive, implied that stronger races would inevitably dominate weaker races. Combined with German nationalism, these racist ideas gave hope to many Germans that the humiliation of the 1920s would be replaced inevitably by a strong Germany that would dominate Europe. ~~Social Darwinism should not be confused with the theories of Charles Darwin, an English naturalist.~~ Nazi ideology was one reason for the success of the Nazi movement because it promised the rebirth of the German nation and Aryan race.

Page 59, Spot the mistake

The paragraph does not get into Level 4 because, although the examples are relevant to the question, their relevance is implicit as there is no explanatory link at the end of the paragraph, linking the examples back to the question.

Page 59, Develop the detail: suggested answer

One reason why the Nazis had emerged as a mass movement by 1932 was that Hitler recruited a series of henchmen who helped to build the party. One of these henchmen was Ernst Röhm, **an ex-military leader**, who developed the SA, **the paramilitary wing of the Nazi Party**, who helped the growth of the party by attacking their political opponents **and by giving a purpose to unemployed young men during the years of the Depression**. Röhm played a key role in the 1920s, **for example, he worked with Hitler to plan and execute the Munich Putsch of November 1923**. Another of Hitler's henchmen was Joseph Goebbels. Goebbels was in charge of propaganda, **and used the Wall Street Crash to his advantage, exploiting the fears of many in rural areas, and giving the Nazi message greater impact**. Hitler's key henchmen were never a threat to his power **because of the *Führerprinzip* established at the 1926 Bamberg Conference**. Thus, the Nazis emerged as a mass movement by 1932 because Hitler recruited talented henchmen, who furthered the appeal of the party and were loyal to the leader.

Page 61, Complete the paragraph: suggested answer

The failure of mainstream politicians during the Depression was clearly one reason why the Nazis had emerged as a mass movement by 1932. In the aftermath of the Depression Müller's Grand Coalition fell apart. A combination of political weakness and constitutional difficulties led to the collapse of Müller's, then Brüning's, then von Papen's, then von Schleicher's governments. Brüning and von Papen attempted to restore order by governing through emergency presidential decrees. Indeed, 44 emergency decrees were issued in 1931 alone. However, mainstream politicians were unable to gain popular support and could not even govern with the full support of the Reichstag. Mainstream politicians also failed to restore economic growth. Brüning's economic schemes were far too small to bring about economic recovery. **In this way, the failure of mainstream politicians in the period 1929–1932 helped the Nazis emerge as a mass movement, because they provided an alternative to the discredited political mainstream.**

Page 67, The flaw in the argument

The argument is flawed because there are errors in its chronology. The Enabling Act was passed after all of the events described in the paragraph. Therefore, it cannot be the cause of these events.

Section 5

Page 77, Summarise the interpretation

Source 1 partially supports the view that the Nazi regime enjoyed widespread popularity in the period 1933–1939 because, although it acknowledges that discontent existed, and increased from the mid-1930s, it states that this opposition was small-scale and ineffective.

Source 2 largely supports the view that the Nazi regime enjoyed widespread popularity in the period 1933–1939 because it argues that a variety of Nazi strategies, including 'propaganda, incentives' and terror, minimised opposition and sustained hopes for a better future. However, it does acknowledge that there was resistance to the Nazi regime from the old elite, Christians and workers, suggesting that popularity was not universal.

Source 3 supports the view that the Nazi regime enjoyed widespread popularity in the period 1933–1939 to a limited extent because it argues that concentration camps and the Gestapo played an important role in diffusing political opposition. Nonetheless, it recognises that the majority of opposition was small-scale.

Page 85, Write the question: suggested answer

How far do you agree that 'it is not altogether false to call Hitler a weak dictator'?

How far do you agree that the chaotic nature of Nazi government led to 'cumulative radicalisation' of policy in the years 1933–1939?

Section 6
Page 93, Spot the mistake

The paragraph does not get into Level 4 because the candidate has mistaken the focus of the question and written an answer concerning the second controversy (how popular and efficient was the Nazi regime in the period 1933–1939?), rather than an answer concerning dissent and opposition during the Second World War.

Page 93, Complete the paragraph: suggested answer

From 1942 to 1944, German morale did remain remarkably high. **Conditions in Germany in the second half of the war were not easy. It was difficult to conceal from the German public that the German army were being beaten on the Russian front. Nonetheless, senior Nazis, aware of the collapse in morale on the home front during the last stages of the First World War, focused consistently on keeping civilian morale high. Therefore, the Nazi authorities ensured 500g of meat per person, extra rations at Christmas, and high levels of propaganda in order to keep civilian morale high. Equally, Hitler's decision not to mobilise women helped maintain morale as many men and women were comforted by the continuation of traditional gender roles.** In this way, German morale remained remarkably high because of Nazi efforts to sustain fighting spirit in the difficult days of 1942–1944.

Page 95, Develop the detail: suggested answer

Left-wing opposition to the Nazi regime failed to have a serious impact on civilian morale during the Second World War. Robert Uhrig established resistance cells **and, by the summer of 1941, there were 89 in Berlin**. Other socialists organised in other localities, **for example, in Hamburg and Mannheim there were socialist Red Patrol groups**. The communists also set up anti-Nazi groups, **such as Rote Kappelle**, to collect information **and distribute anti-Nazi leaflets**. Nonetheless, these groups were largely ineffective. Nazi intelligence services, **such as the Gestapo and the SS**, were successful in breaking up left-wing groups, **for example, William Knöchel's Communist group was broken up in 1943**. The success of Nazi intelligence agencies meant that left-wing groups were unable to get their message across to the public, and therefore these groups had little impact on civilian morale during the war.

Page 97, Eliminate irrelevance

In the early part of the Second World War there is no doubt that the German war economy was highly inefficient. There were some successes. For example, between 1939 and 1941 Germany military expenditure doubled, and by 1941, 55 per cent of the workforce was involved in military production of some sort. However, in spite of these efforts, German productivity lagged behind the productivity of Britain and Russia. The British were able to produce twice as many aircraft in 1941 as the Germans. ~~This was a major embarrassment to Herman Goering, the Chief of the Luftwaffe, who had staked his reputation on the success of his airforce.~~ Additionally, the Russians were able to produce many more tanks than the Germans. ~~However, it should be noted that, before June 1941, Russia and Germany were not at war, having signed a non-aggression pact in 1939.~~ This lack of productivity can be explained by the chaotic organisation of the Nazi war economy, which was characterised by competing, overlapping organisations with no effective co-ordination. ~~Historians have called this type of organisation 'polycratic'.~~ In this way, the German war economy was certainly inefficient in the early years of the Second World War, because German productivity lagged behind that of other major powers.

Page 103, The flaw in the argument

The argument is flawed because it misrepresents what actually happened. Firstly, it overstates the systematic nature of the evolution of policy. Secondly, it ignores counter-evidence, such as the Madagascar Plan, which suggests that the Nazis had no clear idea of how to achieve their anti-Semitic objectives.

Mark scheme

For some of the activities in the book it will be useful to refer to the mark scheme for the unit. Below is the mark scheme for Unit 3.

Part (a)

Level	Marks	Description
1	1–6	• Lacks focus on the question • Limited factual accuracy • Highly generalised *Level 1 answers are highly simplistic, irrelevant, or vague.*
2	7–12	• General points with some focus on the question • Some accurate and relevant supporting evidence *Level 2 answers might tell the story without addressing the question, or address the question without providing supporting examples.*
3	13–18	• General points that focus on the question • Accurate support, but this may be either only partly relevant or lacking detail, or both • Attempted analysis *Level 3 answers attempt to focus on the question, but have significant areas of weakness. For example, the focus on the question may drift, the answer may lack specific examples, or parts of the essay may simply tell the story. Answers which do not deal with factors that are stated in the question cannot achieve higher than Level 3.*
4	19–24	• General points that clearly focus on the question and show understanding of the most important factors involved • Accurate, relevant and detailed supporting evidence • Analysis *Level 4 answers clearly attempt to answer the question and demonstrate a detailed and wide-ranging knowledge of the period studied.*
5	25–30	• As Level 4 • Sustained analysis *Level 5 answers are thorough and detailed. They clearly engage with the question and offer a balanced and carefully reasoned argument, which is sustained throughout the essay.*

Part (b)

A01: Using historical knowledge to form an explanation

Level	Marks	Description
1	1–3	• General points with very limited focus on the question. • Inaccurate supporting evidence. • No integration of sources and own knowledge.
2	4–6	• General points with limited focus on the question. • Accurate and relevant – but generalised – supporting evidence. • Limited attempts to integrate sources and own knowledge.
3	7–10	• General points with focus on the question. • Mostly accurate and relevant supporting evidence. • Some integration of sources and own knowledge.
4	11–13	• General points with strong focus on the question. • Accurate and relevant supporting evidence. • Integration of sources and own knowledge.
5	14–16	• General points with sustained analytical focus on the question. • Accurate and well-selected supporting evidence, showing range of knowledge. • Full integration of sources and own knowledge.

AO2: Analysing source material

1	1–4	• Superficial comprehension of the sources. • Information from the sources is copied or paraphrased. • Extremely limited links between the sources.
2	5–9	• Comprehension of some aspects of the sources. • Information from the sources is summarised and used to provide a simple answer to the question. • Some use of the sources in combination.
3	10–14	• The main aspects of the sources are analysed. • Evidence from the sources is selected to support and challenge the view expressed in the question. • The sources are used in combination.
4	15–19	• The sources are interpreted with confidence. • The interpretations of the sources are used to debate the view expressed in the question. • The sources are used in combination. • The essay reaches a judgement based on the interpretations of the sources and own knowledge.
5	20–24	• The sources are interpreted with confidence and discrimination. • The interpretations of the sources are used to debate the view expressed in the question. • The sources are used in combination. • The essay reaches a fully substantiated judgement based on the interpretations of the sources and own knowledge.